PHOTOSHOP®
Finishing Touches

Dave Cross

Senior Developer, Education and Curriculum
National Association of Photoshop Professionals

Photoshop® Finishing Touches Team

CREATIVE DIRECTOR
Felix Nelson

TECHNICAL EDITORS
Kim Doty
Cindy Snyder

PRODUCTION EDITOR
Kim Gabriel

PRODUCTION MANAGER
Dave Damstra

COVER DESIGN &
CREATIVE CONCEPTS
Jessica Maldonado

COVER PHOTOS
COURTESY OF
Dave Cross
iStockphoto.com

Published by
Peachpit

Copyright © 2007 by Kelby Corporate Management, Inc.

First edition: July 2006

Composed in Myriad Pro (Adobe Systems Incorporated), Warnock Pro (Adobe Systems Incorporated), and Savoye LET Plain (Esselte Letraset Ltd.) by NAPP Publishing.

Trademarks
All terms mentioned in this book that are known to be trademarks or service marks have been appropriately capitalized. Peachpit cannot attest to the accuracy of this information. Use of a term in the book should not be regarded as affecting the validity of any trademark or service mark.

Macintosh is a registered trademark of Apple Computer.
Windows is a registered trademark of Microsoft Corporation.
Photoshop and Illustrator are registered trademarks of Adobe Systems Incorporated.

Warning and Disclaimer
This book is designed to provide information about Photoshop CS2 tips. Every effort has been made to make this book as complete and as accurate as possible, but no warranty of fitness is implied.

The information is provided on an as-is basis. The author and Peachpit shall have neither liability nor responsibility to any person or entity with respect to any loss or damages arising from the information contained in this book or from the use of the discs or programs that may accompany it.

ISBN 0-321-44166-4

9 8 7 6 5 4 3 2 1

Printed and bound in the United States of America

www.peachpit.com
www.scottkelbybooks.com

I dedicate this book to inspiration, since
that's a big part of the creative process,
and the things that inspire me: music,
photography, teaching, and my family.

acknowledgments

I'm a firm believer in the whole life-long learning concept. One of my favorite things about working in the Photoshop industry is that you literally never stop learning new things. I feel very privileged to work in an environment where I'm surrounded by people who constantly teach me things, and remind me about stuff I occasionally forget.

Scott Kelby has taught me a ton of things, and I'm not just talking about the obvious clever uses of Photoshop, although he has certainly done that. Scott reminds me every day through his actions and his personality that people are the most important thing. That includes the people you work with, the people in your family and circle of friends, and in our case, the people who are members of the National Association of Photoshop Professionals. Everything Scott does reflects not only his passion for Photoshop, but also his never-ending belief in doing things as best as they can be done and his passion for making people happy, and I am a better person because of his influence.

If there's anyone who provides me with my daily dose of reminders, it's Dave Moser. It's part of his mission to remind me about upcoming deadlines and the next big project (more likely, projects). But like Scott, Dave's actions speak louder than words, and he reminds me of the importance of giving it everything you have, and always taking things up a notch. In his own unique way, Dave is encouraging and incredibly supportive and I am a better man thanks to him.

Felix Nelson unknowingly reminds me that although I know a thing or two about Photoshop, he can still bring me back down to earth with his amazing Photoshop abilities. Luckily for us, he is more than happy to share the wealth and pull the rest of us along for the ride. I also consider myself very lucky that Felix has assembled an amazing team that made this book a reality. Thanks to Jessica Maldonado for the book cover and design concepts, Dave Damstra for his kickin' layouts, and the editing team of Kim Doty and Cindy Snyder, who always questioned, poked, prodded, and made this book better. Thanks also to Kim Gabriel for her typically stellar job of keeping us all on track.

(This is my third time writing an acknowledgment for a book, and I stand by the same statement I made in the other two: It would be easier to include the entire company roster in this section because each and every one plays a vital role in the day-to-day stuff we do at KW Media. Thanks folks, each of you.)

Working with the fine folks at Peachpit Press helps me to remember the importance of communication and discussion. Right from the get-go, my friends at Peachpit have been a great help in making suggestions that helped make this a better book. Although there are many people who I know play an active role, I have had the most direct dealings with Ted Waitt and Rachel Tiley, so I thank them in the name of all the people I don't know at Peachpit.

I am very lucky to know and work side-by-side with the best Photoshop teachers and writers in the industry. Through Photoshop World I have gotten to know, learn from, and be inspired by people like Ben Willmore, Jack Davis, Bert Monroy, Katrin Eismann, Eddie Tapp, Julieanne Kost, Deke McClelland…again, it would be easier for you to check the instructor list at www.photoshopworld.com to see all the people that I should recognize.

A number of the techniques in the book are based in part on ideas from Dan Margulis, Eddie Tapp, Scott Kelby, Matt Kloskowski, and Katrin Eismann, and I thank them for their inspiration.

As I work side-by-side with Matt Kloskowski, I am reminded that you should always take great pride in what you do, and do it with a smile. I've never worked with a guy who so clearly loves what he does—and does it with a great big smile and positive attitude all the time. It's really amazing and inspiring, and he unknowingly pushes me to approach our crazy nuthouse workplace with the same positive attitude and sense of fun.

When my kids were little ones, I never really thought that I'd be the one learning from them, but sure enough, they've taught me volumes over the years. Michael reminds me how important it is to create a balance between the commitment to get things done and having a wonderful laid-back demeanor. He's an awesome student, athlete, and friend with an amazing ability to put things into perspective—I'm still trying to learn that skill.

Through her daily approach to life, Stephanie constantly reminds me of the importance of being passionate about things. She never ceases to amaze me with her drive to get things done. Once she put her mind to it, she was determined to head off to Canada, get her own place, and start college, which she has done with great success. I'm just about bursting with pride.

If I were allowed another few pages for this section of the book, I'd go into great detail about the many, many things my beautiful wife Marlene has taught me, and continues to teach me every day. She is my inspiration in so many ways and is my motivation to be a success. She strives for excellence in every single thing she does, and it's impossible not to be in awe of what she does and not be motivated by her approach. Marlene is the ultimate believer in the importance of family, and our extended family has grown closer as a direct result of her expressions of love. I can't really put into words how much my world revolves around her, and how much better a man I am thanks to her love.

All in all, I consider myself a very lucky man to have such a wonderful family, to work doing something I love, and to be inspired, motivated, and taught by my circle of co-workers and friends.

about the author

DAVE CROSS

Dave Cross is Senior Developer, Education and Curriculum, for the National Association of Photoshop Professionals and is involved in all aspects of the training that is provided to NAPP members, including the content of seminars, conferences, and workbooks. He also creates the very popular weekly QuickTime-based tutorials that appear on the members' website. Dave is an Adobe Certified Instructor in Photoshop CS2 and Illustrator CS2, and is a Certified Technical Trainer.

Prior to joining NAPP, Dave lived in Canada and trained thousands of users across North America. He has been using and teaching Adobe Illustrator and Adobe Photoshop since their original versions, starting in 1987. Dave is the author of *The Photoshop CS2 Help Desk Book* and co-author of *Illustrator CS2 Killer Tips*.

Dave writes the "Classic Photoshop Effects" and "Beginners' Workshop" columns for *Photoshop User* magazine, teaches at the Photoshop World Conference & Expo, and is the Lead Instructor for the Photoshop Seminar Tour. He also is featured on a series of DVDs, such as *Best of Photoshop User*, *Photoshop CS2 for Beginners*, and *Photoshop CS2 Layer Techniques*, and is a cohost of the *Adobe® Photoshop® TV* video podcast.

In his spare time, Dave is the Graphics/News Editor for *Layers* magazine, and enjoys freaking out his Florida co-workers by wearing shorts to work every day, simply "because he can." Dave lives in Odessa, Florida, with his wife, Marlene, and children, Stephanie and Michael.

section I *key concepts*

Stroke
Width: 2 px
Color:

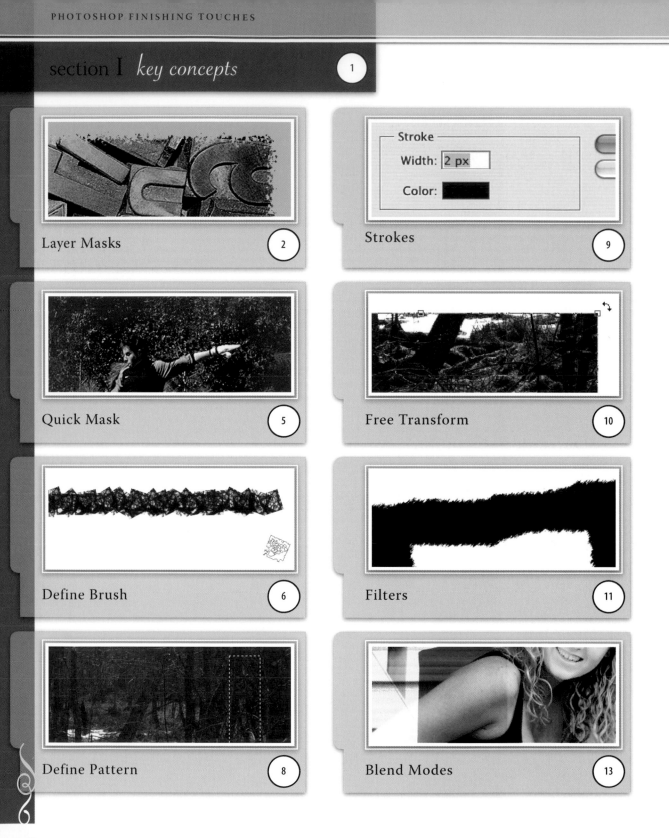

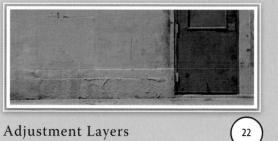
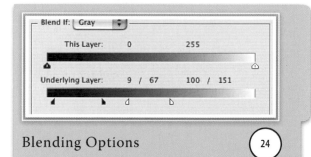

section II *frames & border effects* 39

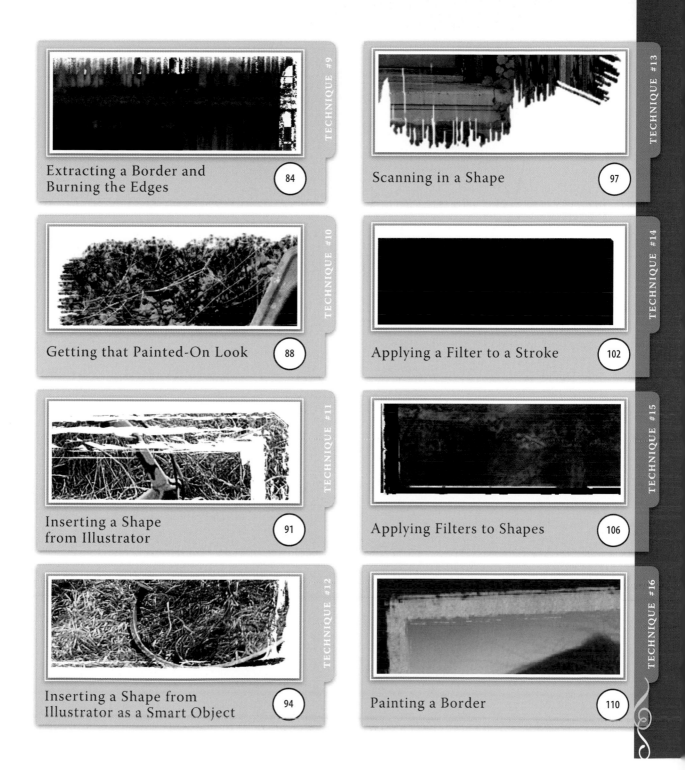

section II *frames & border effects*

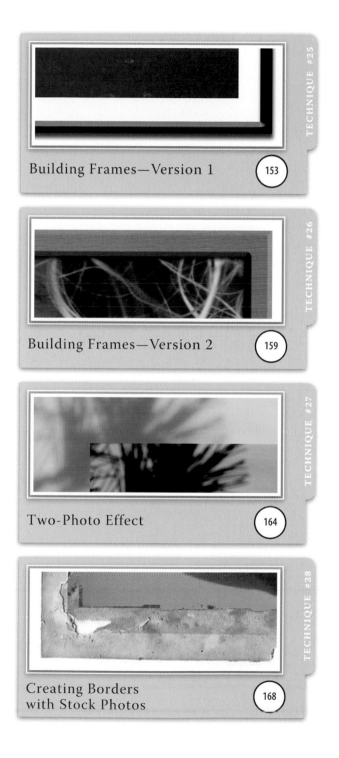

section III *color & artistic effects* 175

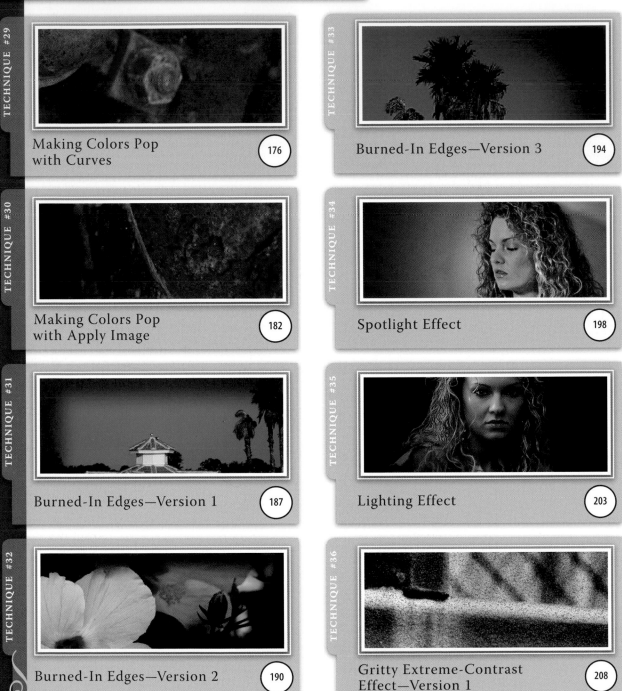

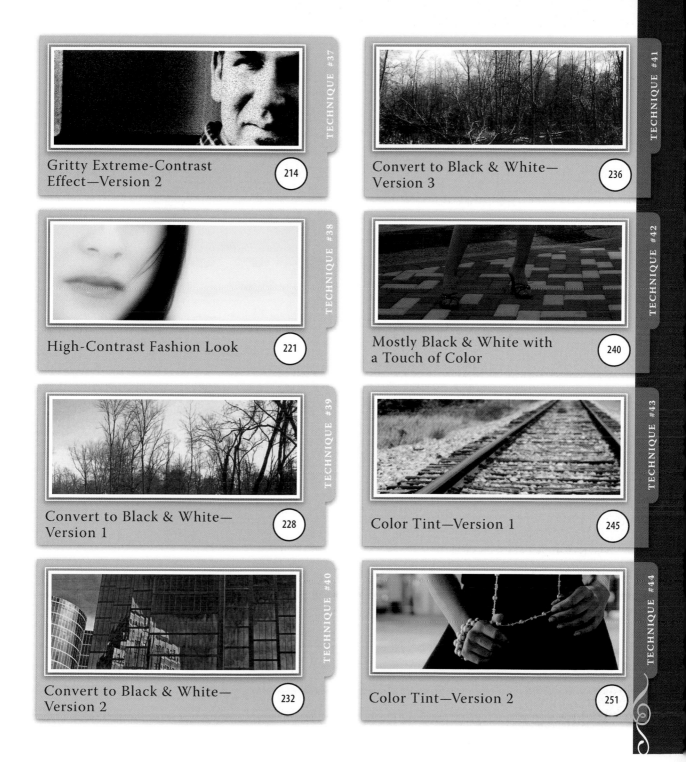

section III *color & artistic effects*

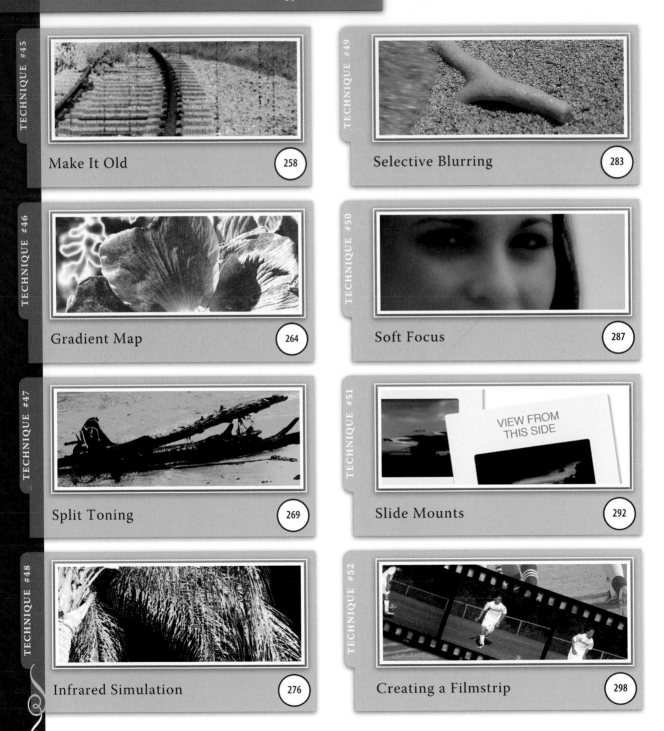

section IV *presenting your work* 317

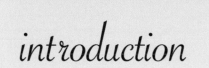

introduction

introduction

I love to cook. Okay, so I'm guessing that you weren't expecting that opening remark at the start of a Photoshop book, but stick with me for a few moments, would you? When I first started cooking, I had several old, reliable cookbooks that I used religiously; if I had a dish in mind, I would look it up, check the ingredients, and start carefully following the instructions. Over time my confidence grew, and I started experimenting and trying my own variations. These days my many cookbooks have been relegated to answering questions like, "How many minutes per pound for a rib roast?"

Can you see where this is going yet? Here we go: Back in Photoshop 2 days, my ever-present book was *The Photoshop Wow! Book*, by Jack Davis and Linnea Dayton. I would look through the book, find a cool-looking technique, and start carefully following the steps. If Step Five told me to change the blend mode to Overlay, then I would, without question. The more I used the book, the more I realized that I was getting pretty darn good…at following instructions. This is not to say that there was anything wrong with the book, far from it. I was using the book incorrectly by blindly following instructions without taking the time to experiment. Things really changed for me when I started being a little more curious and asking myself things like, "If Overlay mode works, what would Screen mode do?" So I'd try it, relying heavily on the good old Undo command. The more I did that, the more I started to understand why things worked the way they did, and was more willing to start cooking up my own concoctions. That's what I'm going to suggest you do, too.

There are a few things that I think make this book a little different. First, I'm assuming a certain level of knowledge of Photoshop. I'll tell you to "fill with white," rather than saying "from the Edit menu, choose Fill, and in the dialog, choose White." If a technique calls for a layer mask, I won't explain in great detail what a mask does— at least not in the technique itself. Instead, that's what the Key Concepts section is for: as a reference, if you're not sure what the technique is referring to. Most of the techniques list the key concepts used in that particular method, so if you need a little help understanding a step, check out the explanation in the Key Concepts section.

If you like, you can start out by reading the entire Key Concepts section, but it's not absolutely necessary. I designed this book to be a "jump in anywhere" kind of deal.

Another important difference in how this book operates is the Table of Contents. As I was writing the techniques, I was calling them things like "Apply a Filter to a Stroke," and realized that names like this are not the most descriptive things in the world. Looking in a Table of Contents and seeing "Color Tint—Version 1" and "Color Tint—Version 2" probably wouldn't help you decide which technique was for you. Instead, we created a visual Table of Contents, where you can look at samples of the techniques and go to the appropriate page. Quick and easy.

Perhaps the most important difference is the expectation I have of you: I want you to experiment! Just like the cook in me who started experimenting once I had the basic idea, you need to take these techniques and run with them. I deliberately don't give you fixed settings for filters and adjustment layers, instead providing examples and variations that should get your explorative senses tingling. The permutations and combinations really should be endless, but only if you buy into the concept and start playing. There are some similarities between techniques, including a few filters or blend modes that are used pretty often—but that doesn't mean that you should only use those specific steps. Be an explorer! There is nothing that would make me happier than to have someone tell me, "My edge effect looks nothing like the one in the book… and I love it!"

In fact, you really can show me the way you use the techniques in the book—just go to www.photoshopfinishingtouches.com to share your work, and maybe learn a few new ideas along the way.

By the way, I made it my goal to use only my photos in this book, and with the exception of a couple of photos from my daughter, Stephanie, and a few stock photos I used as frames, I've managed to do that. I'm sure that I could have found some images with more impact or more variety, but one of the underlying concepts of this book is to add finishing touches to your own images, so I decided to set an example by using my personal images. I gotta say it certainly was easy to get motivated to experiment on photos that I shot.

So that's it—the recipe to success with this book is to jump in and start experimenting. So preheat your computer, put on your chef's hat, and start cookin'!

I

key concepts

You can start here, read this section when you need it, or ignore it completely. How's that for an easy-to-get-along-with book? If you read the book introduction, you'll already know that this Key Concepts section is intended as a reference you can use if and when you need it (if you didn't read the introduction, this Key Concepts section is intended as a reference you can use if and when you need it).

So it's up to you: read through this entire section, or jump right into the individual techniques and come back here if you need to. Just about all the techniques start with icons that represent the key concepts used in their steps, so if you need some clarification or background information, you can come back here for a little help.

Stay? Go? It's up to you…

layer masks

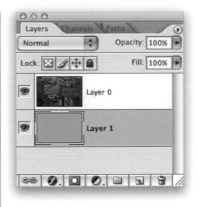

One of the ways we'll create effects that are both highly editable and potentially transferable is by using layer masks. In contrast to deleting or erasing portions of the image, a layer mask allows you to hide areas of an image, meaning those pixels are never deleted, and can always be shown again.

Creating a Layer Mask

In this example, I double-clicked on the Background layer and renamed it (this is necessary since you cannot add a layer mask to the Background layer). Then I added a new layer, filled it with a color, and then clicked-and-dragged the new layer below my image layer. By clicking on the Add Layer Mask icon at the bottom of the Layers palette, a layer mask was added to the image layer. At first nothing changes since, by default, the layer mask is added in Reveal All mode, which means the entire layer is visible. By painting on the layer mask with black, I was able to hide portions of the image layer.

One of the main principles of using layer masks is the role of black and white: black hides, white reveals. (And as we'll see, shades of gray will have a partial effect, making pixels somewhat hidden or somewhat visible, depending on the shade of gray.)

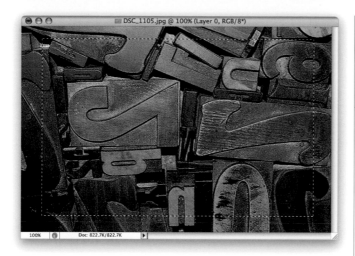

Another way to create a layer mask is to start with a selection. Here I used the Rectangular Marquee tool to select a large portion of the image. As soon as I click on the Add Layer Mask icon, the selected area remains visible while the areas that were not selected are hidden. Another way to think of this would be that the selected area was filled with white while the non-selected area was filled with black.

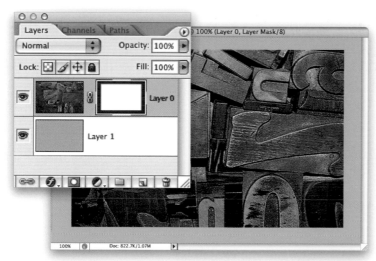

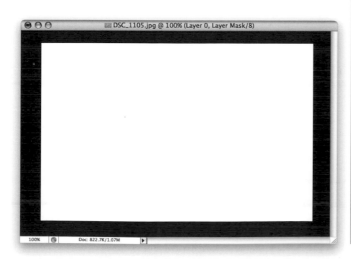

Working with Layer Masks

It's important to remember that once you've added a layer mask, you'll have two elements you can work with: the layer itself or the mask. You simply have to make sure that you click on the appropriate thumbnail in the Layers palette (look for the black border around the thumbnail to indicate that it is selected). To edit the layer mask, you "paint" with black, white, or shades of gray. This can be done using the Brush tool, by making a selection and filling it with color, or painting with the Gradient tool. You can also apply filters to the mask that will in turn affect the areas that are hidden or shown.

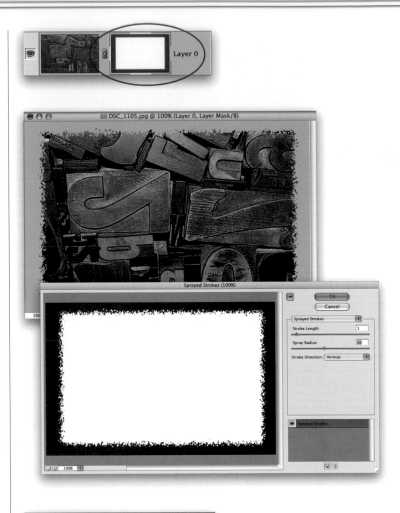

By default, the layer and its layer mask are linked (as indicated by the Link icon between the two thumbnails in the Layers palette). This means that when you have either one selected and you use the Move tool to click-and-drag, both the layer and the mask will move together. You may also choose to unlink the mask from the layer (by clicking on the Link icon to remove it) so that you can move the layer independently from its mask. At any time, you can re-link the layer and the layer mask by clicking between the two thumbnails.

Some techniques in this book will call for you to paste pixels onto an existing layer mask, which requires an extra step. That is, if you simply copy some pixels and then paste, a new layer will be created. In order to paste onto an existing layer mask, you'll have to view the mask rather than the layer. You do this by pressing-and-holding the Option key (PC: Alt key) as you click on the layer mask thumbnail. Then the Paste command will indeed paste onto the mask (rather than creating a new layer).

If you want to view a layer without the effect of its mask, press-and-hold the Shift key, click on the layer mask thumbnail, and the layer mask will be hidden (indicated by the big red X). To make the layer mask take effect again, just click on the mask thumbnail.

quick mask

Getting a Different View

Quick Mask mode provides an alternate way of viewing a selection—as a colored overlay, rather than the selection edges (aka: marching ants). Here's an example of a selection that was created by making multiple selections with the Rectangular Marquee tool (with the Shift key held down). By clicking on the Quick Mask icon (at the bottom of the Toolbox), the view is changed to Quick Mask mode where the non-selected areas are indicated by a colored overlay. (*Note:* You can also press the letter Q to switch between Quick Mask and Standard modes.)

Editing in Quick Mask mode uses a similar concept to working on a layer mask—paint with white to add to the selection and paint with black to deselect. You can also apply filters in Quick Mask mode. Here I used the Gaussian Blur filter to blur the edges of the selection. This is a great way to add the equivalent of feathering but with a preview.

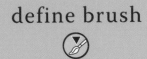

define brush

Making Your Own Brushes

We'll be using a bunch of techniques that involve making a new brush. Okay, technically, it's called defining a brush preset, but many people refer to it as making a brush since it also can involve tweaking the settings in the Brushes palette. You start with a photo or paint a shape, make a selection, and then choose Edit>Define Brush Preset. Here I made a small selection in a photo (shown in Quick Mask mode, just so it's easier to see). After choosing Edit>Define Brush Preset, I named my brush and then clicked OK. In order to make the new brush more interesting, I used the Brushes palette (docked in the Palette Well by default) to change some settings. I used the Brush Tip Shape options to rotate the brush slightly and increase the spacing. In the Shape Dynamics options, I changed the Size Jitter to 3% and increased the Angle Jitter to 29%.

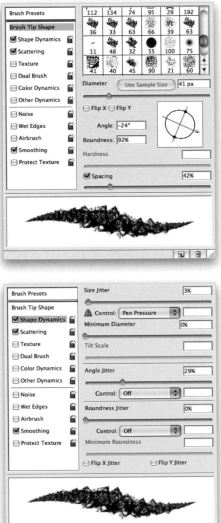

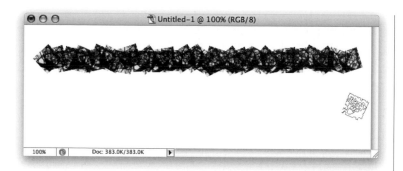

I created a new blank document and, using the Brush tool with my new brush shape, I clicked once on one side of the new document. Then while pressing-and-holding the Shift key, I clicked on the other side of the document. This painted a straight line but as you can see, the brush rotated and changed size slightly based on my settings in the Brushes palette.

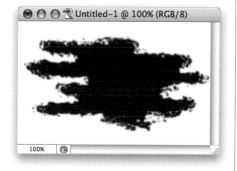

Another way to make a brush shape is to start with a blank document and create a painted shape. Here I used a standard brush to paint a few lines in black, applied several filters (Motion Blur, Glass, and Dry Brush), and then finished it off with Threshold and a little Gaussian Blur. (I'm deliberately not giving you step-by-step instructions here because I want you to start experimenting and making brushes.) Once you've created a shape you like, again use Edit>Define Brush Preset to create the brush shape, and then if you like, tweak the settings in the Brushes palette.

As we'll see throughout the book, this type of brush can be used to paint borders, stroke a path, or paint on a layer mask.

define pattern

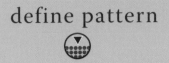

Making Your Own Pattern

Another tool at our disposal is a pattern—either the ones that are built into Photoshop or patterns that you create. Patterns can be incorporated into brush settings, used to fill a selection, or you can paint with a pattern using the Pattern Stamp tool. Creating a pattern is as simple as making a selection and choosing Edit>Define Pattern. Name the pattern and it's ready for use. You can also get some interesting results by defining a pattern from an entire photo—just use Edit>Define Pattern without making a selection first.

We'll make use of custom patterns in some pretty interesting ways!

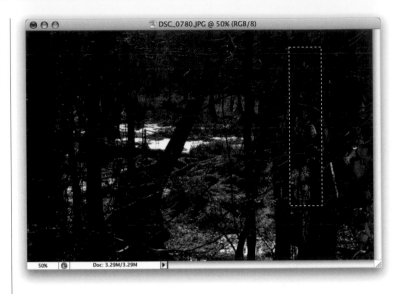

Color Overlay...
Gradient Overlay...
Pattern Overlay...
Stroke...

p	File	Edit	Image	Layer	Select	Filter	View

Undo Load Selection ⌘Z
Step Forward ⇧⌘Z
Step Backward ⌥⌘Z

Fade... ⇧⌘F

Cut ⌘X
Copy ⌘C
Copy Merged ⇧⌘C
Paste ⌘V
Paste Into ⇧⌘V
Clear

Check Spelling...
Find and Replace Text...

Fill... ⇧F5
Stroke...

Free Transform ⌘T

Stroke

Stroke
Width: 2 px
Color:

OK
Cancel

Location
◉ Inside ○ Center ○ Outside

Blending
Mode: Normal
Opacity: 100 %
☐ Preserve Transparency

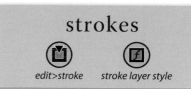

strokes

edit>stroke   stroke layer style

Edit>Stroke vs. Stroke Layer Style

There are two ways to apply a stroke—as a layer style or by using Edit>Stroke—and as you can probably guess, there are advantages to each. If you have objects on a separate layer and want to add a stroke, then using a layer style has two distinct advantages: you can edit the stroke at any time, and the stroke automatically resizes as you resize the object on the layer. On the other hand, you cannot apply a filter to a layer style, so if that's one of the options you're looking for, it's better to use Edit>Stroke.

Regardless of which method you use to add a stroke, there is one factor that probably won't change, and that is using Inside as the position of the stroke. The reason is, using Center or Outside as the stroke position results in a stroke with slightly rounded corners, while the Inside position will create sharp corners. (Oh, by the way, one of the quirks of the Stroke layer style is that it continually defaults to rather odd settings: a red stroke positioned Outside. Chances are, you won't find yourself using that setting very often—or at all!)

free transform

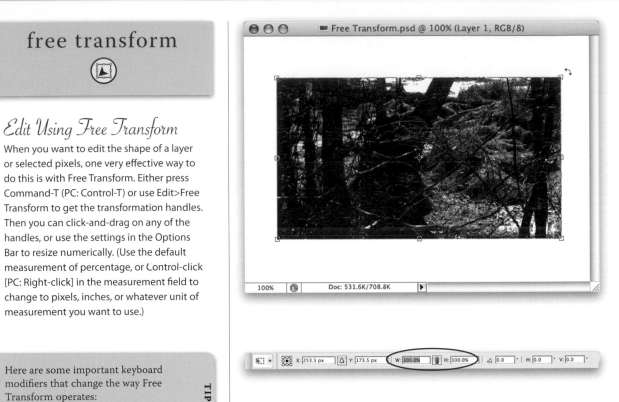

Edit Using Free Transform

When you want to edit the shape of a layer or selected pixels, one very effective way to do this is with Free Transform. Either press Command-T (PC: Control-T) or use Edit>Free Transform to get the transformation handles. Then you can click-and-drag on any of the handles, or use the settings in the Options Bar to resize numerically. (Use the default measurement of percentage, or Control-click [PC: Right-click] in the measurement field to change to pixels, inches, or whatever unit of measurement you want to use.)

TIP

Here are some important keyboard modifiers that change the way Free Transform operates:

Shift: Keeps the transformation proportional.

Option (PC: Alt): Transforms from the center outwards.

Command (PC: Control): Transforms the one handle you click on.

Command-Shift (PC: Control-Shift): Skews selection.

Command-Option-Shift (PC: Control-Alt-Shift): Creates perspective.

Move your mouse just outside the corner handles to get the Rotate cursor.

Once you're finished transforming, press Return (PC: Enter) to "confirm" the transformation. Press Escape to cancel out of Free Transform.

Filter	View	Window	Help
Last Filter			⌘F

Extract...	⌥⌘X
Filter Gallery...	
Liquify...	⇧⌘X
Pattern Maker...	⌥⇧⌘X
Vanishing Point...	⌥⌘V

Artistic	▶	Colored Pencil...
Blur	▶	Cutout...
Brush Strokes	▶	Dry Brush...
Distort	▶	Film Grain...
Noise	▶	Fresco...
Pixelate	▶	Neon Glow...
Render	▶	Paint Daubs...
Sharpen	▶	Palette Knife...
Sketch	▶	Plastic Wrap...

filters

Creating Effects with Filters

Although I personally have no current plans to do so, there could be an entire book written just on using filters. We'll use filters in lots of different ways throughout this book, but rather than attempt to discuss them all in great detail, I thought I'd give you a few guidelines about using filters (in part because I want you to experiment with different filters and see what you get). So here are my general guidelines for using filters:

1. Given a choice, use filters with an ellipsis (…) after the name as those filters will provide a dialog with options—filters without the ellipsis will run using some predefined setting.

2. If a filter has a Preview checkbox or preview window, take advantage of them! Turn the Preview checkbox off and on to see the before and after—*before* you commit to anything. You can also see a before and after by using the preview window: click-and-hold in the window to see the original; let go to see the results of your current settings.

3. If nothing is selected, a filter will apply itself to the entire image or layer, so if you want to restrict the effects of a filter, make a selection first.

4. To reapply the last filter that you used—with the same settings—press Command-F (PC: Control-F). To open the dialog of the last filter you used so you can change the settings, press Command-Option-F (PC: Control-Alt-F).

Motion Blur

OK

Cancel

☑ Preview

⊟ 100% ⊞

Angle: -39 °

Distance: 16 pixels

5. If you apply a filter and the effect is too intense, use Edit>Fade and lower the opacity of the filter so that the original image shows through. You can also experiment with the blend modes in the Fade dialog.

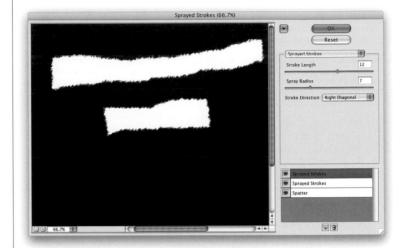

6. Many filters open in the Filter Gallery—without a doubt one of the greatest ways to experiment. In the Filter Gallery, you can add multiple filters (even more than one of the same filter) and experiment with changing the order or showing and hiding the filter layers. Just remember that although this resembles working with the Layers palette, the Filter Gallery does not allow you to go back and change the results. Instead, if you don't like the results of your filter gallery, Undo, and press Command-Option-F (PC: Control-Alt-F) to open the Filter Gallery with the same filters—then you can change settings, alter the order of the filters, etc.

7. Although this won't always be an option in the techniques we're using, one way to have a little more control over a filter is by duplicating the image (or layer), applying the filter, and then using the layer opacity control to lower the opacity of the filtered version so the original shows through. (This is similar in concept to using the Fade command, but the duplicated layer gives you ongoing flexibility as opposed to Fade, which is a one-shot deal.)

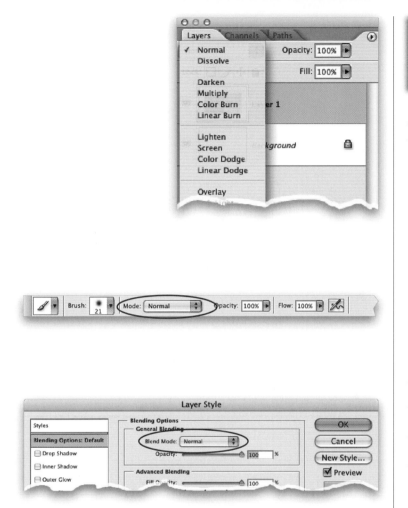

blend modes

Changing Blend Modes

There are a number of places in Photoshop where you'll come across blend modes: the Layers palette, the Options Bar for various painting tools, certain layer styles, some adjustment commands, and even in some brush settings. Blend modes have an effect on the way the color used by a tool or layer interacts with the colors of the layer(s) below. Some people have a burning desire to understand how each blend mode works so they can predict what will happen. If you're one of those people, then you're in for a big disappointment as I have no such desire to know this level of detail, or write about it. (Check the Photoshop Help files or many other fine books such as *Photoshop CS2 Studio Techniques* by Ben Willmore for full explanations of blend modes.) In my typical cut-to-the-chase manner of working in Photoshop, I think it's simpler to know the main blend modes you're likely to use, and a shortcut to help you browse through the different blend modes.

First, the shortcut: To scroll through the blend modes, press Shift–+ (plus sign). If you have a painting tool selected, you'll change the blend mode of that tool; if you have the Move tool (or any non-painting tool) selected, you'll scroll through the blend modes for the current active layer. To scroll backwards through the blend modes, press Shift– - (minus sign).

Here are the blend modes you are likely to use the most. Of course, you may use others in your experiments but my surveys show that people use these blend modes more than others (in my world, "survey" means "this is what people tell me, and what I see the most in tutorials").

Shown here are the two layers I'll use to illustrate the effects of the blend modes: the background layer and the top layer (the blend mode of this top layer is the one that is changing).

The background layer

Normal: The top layer completely covers the underlying layer, with no interaction of any kind.

The top layer

Dissolve

Dissolve: Combines the two layers using a random pattern of pixels—use a lower opacity to see the results.

Darken

Darken: Colors on the top layer are only applied where they are darker than the colors on the underlying layer.

Multiply: Multiplies the layers together to produce darker colors (except for white, which disappears). Ben Willmore describes this as printing one image on top of another on an ink jet printer (not that you should do that!).

Multiply

Color Burn: Similar to Multiply, but adds more saturation to the underlying layer.

Color Burn

Screen

Screen: Multiplies the inverse of the layers together to produce lighter colors (except for black, which disappears). Has been compared to projecting light through two different slides at the same time.

Overlay

Overlay: Darkens the shadows (like Multiply) and lightens the highlights (like Screen). Gray has no effect.

Soft Light: Lightens the underlying layer if the top layer is lighter than 50% gray, and darkens the underlying layer if the top layer is darker than 50% gray.

Soft Light

Color: Combines the hue and saturation of the top layer with the luminance (brightness values) of the underlying layer.

Color

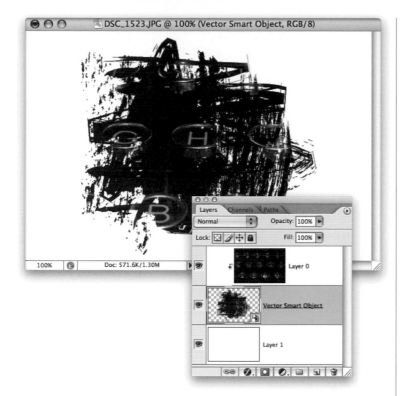

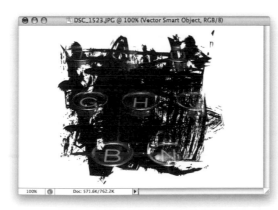

from illustrator to photoshop

Using Illustrator Shapes in Photoshop

A very effective way to create interesting borders and shapes we'll use in some of the book's techniques is available if you also own Adobe Illustrator. It involves using Illustrator's built-in tools and brushes to create unique shapes, and then using those shapes in Photoshop as a layer mask, clipping mask, or border. Illustrator has many options for creating a wide range of looks, using the built-in brushes or by creating your own shapes. Depending on how you use these shapes in Photoshop, they can be scaled quite dramatically without losing quality.

After creating a basic path in Illustrator and applying a brush to the path, you copy the path and paste it into a Photoshop document. Several options are available in Photoshop's Paste As dialog, each of which has advantages and disadvantages:

Smart Object: Creates a link in Photoshop to the original Illustrator artwork. This means you can easily update the artwork "on the fly." This works best when you create a layer clipping mask, as shown above.

Double-clicking on the Vector Smart Object takes you back to Illustrator where you can edit the object. Close and save the document, switch back to the Photoshop document, and the Smart Object automatically updates (which in turn updates the effect of the clipping mask). Smart Objects also can be resized without losing quality.

Disadvantage: You cannot apply filters to a Smart Object, nor can you use it as a layer mask unless you rasterize the Smart Object (which pretty much defeats the purpose of using a Smart Object).

Pixels: Creates a pixel (rasterized) version of the vector artwork that can be used as a border or in a mask. When you first paste as pixels you'll get handles that you use to scale the Illustrator artwork to the appropriate size.

Disadvantage: There is no link to the original artwork and you cannot make the pixels larger without losing quality.

Path: Creates a work path in the Photoshop document, which preserves the vector nature of the Illustrator artwork (as a path that can be edited). That path can be used to create a selection that can be filled and used as a border or in a layer mask.

Disadvantage: It's not really a disadvantage, but it can be a little tricky to work with the Paths and Layers palettes to get the result you want.

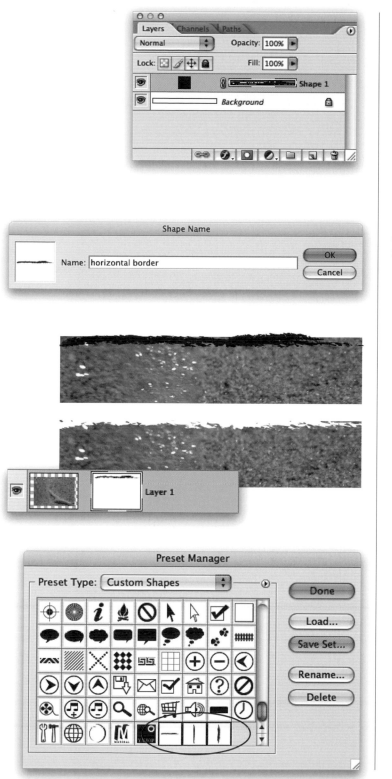

Shape Layer: Creates a Shape layer that preserves the vector shape, which can be edited, and also can be turned into a custom shape that can be sized by dragging. To create a custom shape, click on the Shape layer's vector mask thumbnail, choose Edit>Define Custom Shape, and name the shape. Then you can drag with the Custom Shape tool to either create a border or a layer mask. (When you define a custom shape, it remains built into Photoshop unless you reset the Custom Shape Picker.)

Disadvantage: No real disadvantages here, but it is important to create a backup of your custom shapes using Edit>Preset Manager and the Save Set option.

adjustment layers

Making Editable Adjustments

With a few exceptions, most of the key adjustments you can apply to an image can be done in two ways: from the Image menu under Adjustments, or as an adjustment layer. Very simply, an adjustment layer gives you the ability to return to the original adjustment dialog to make further changes, whereas the Image>Adjustments commands do not. Here's a comparison of using Levels in two different ways.

First, I pressed Command-L (PC: Control-L) and made an adjustment to the photo. Looking at the Layers palette, it's clear that the adjustment was made directly to the Background layer. If I were to save that document and then open it weeks later attempting to tweak the Levels command, I'd get a Levels histogram that looked something like the one you see here. This kind of histogram indicates that changes have already been made to the image, and although it's theoretically possible to make further changes, it is challenging—even if all you want to do is return to the original image.

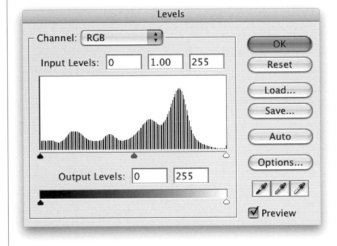

In contrast, choosing Levels from the Create New Adjustment Layer icon's pop-up menu (at the bottom of the Layers palette) adds a new layer to the document. At any time, I can double-click on the adjustment layer's thumbnail to re-open the Levels dialog and get the original dialog, just as I left it. This allows for ongoing adjustments—as long as you save a layered document that includes the adjustment layer(s).

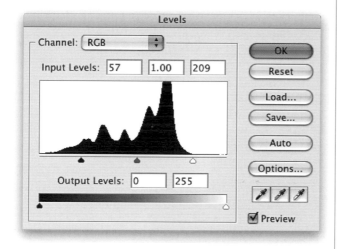

The other advantages of an adjustment layer include the ability to hide it, delete it completely, change its opacity or blend mode, or include more than one of the same type of adjustment. So, am I suggesting that you should *always* use an adjustment layer? Not necessarily, but I would suggest (insist?) that you at least *consider* using an adjustment layer to determine if that would be the best way to go.

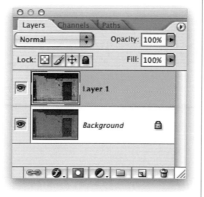

One last thing: there are a few types of adjustments that are not available as an adjustment layer (such as Shadow/Highlight, Match Color, and Exposure). In those cases, the next best thing to using an adjustment layer is to duplicate the Background layer and apply these commands to the copy of the Background. That way you can at least experiment with opacity and blend modes or throw away the layer and start over again.

blending options

Using the Blend If Sliders

Not to be confused with blend modes, Blending Options appears at the top of the Layer Style dialog and controls the way that layers interact with each other. To illustrate this, I have taken a photo and added a layer that has squares filled with black, white, 50% gray, and gradients.

Double-clicking beside the layer name will open the Layer Style dialog with the focus on Blending Options: Default. (You can also Control-click [PC: Right-click] on the layer and choose Blending Options at the top of the contextual menu.) The two sliders under Blend If are the controls we'll use to change the interaction of the layers.

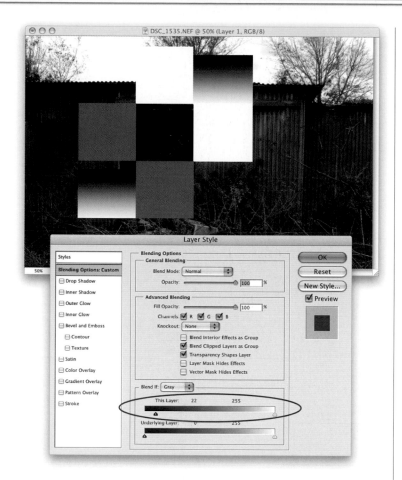

Using the top slider called This Layer means (strangely enough) that you will be affecting the current layer. Here I dragged the black slider slightly to the right. That made anything black on the layer become see-through, showing the layer below. Notice how the black portion of the gradient boxes also became see-through.

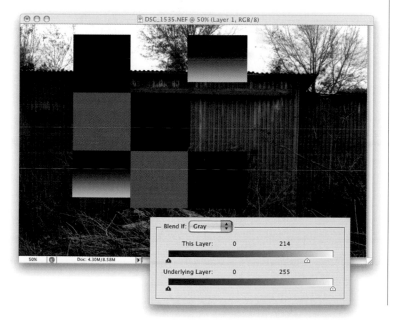

In this case, I took the white slider under This Layer and pulled it in to the left, making the white areas of the layer see-through. Since the boxes were pure white, they disappeared as soon as I moved the slider even a small amount. Again, take note of the white portions of the gradient boxes and how those areas were affected. If the layer contains white and shades that are progressively darker than white, the further I drag the white slider, the more shades will be affected.

One of the potential problems with these sliders is the tendency to get very obvious edges where the colors become see-through. To fix this, press-and-hold the Option key (PC: Alt key) and click on the slider to split it into two. Now, as the two halves of the slider are moved, it will create a smoother transition on the edges.

The same concept applies to the Underlying Layer section: as you drag the sliders, the dark or light areas of the bottom layer start to show through the top layer. Here I dragged the black slider to the right to force dark areas of the Background layer to show through the top layer.

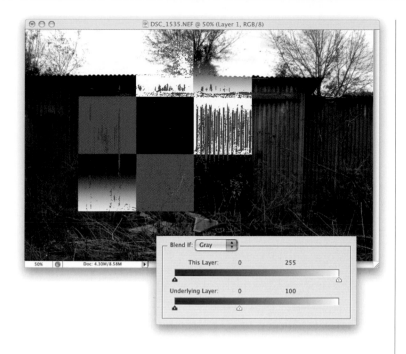

In the next case, the white slider was moved way to the left to make the few lighter areas of the shed show through the squares.

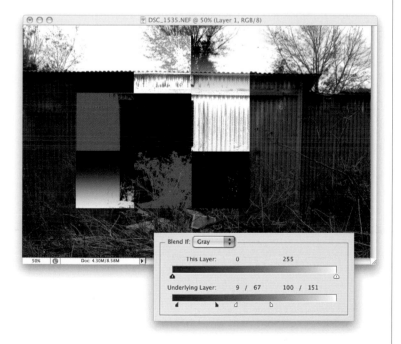

In an example of what will often be your strategy, I then split the two sliders and played with the sides of both the white and black sliders until I got the result I wanted.

Another very effective way to use the Blend If sliders is with an adjustment layer. Here I applied a Color Balance adjustment layer to change the look of the photo. Then I Control-clicked (PC: Right-clicked) on the adjustment layer, chose Blending Options, and used the methods previously described to change the areas of the photo that were affected by the adjustment layer.

layer styles

Adding Editable, Scalable Effects

If you want to add a little something to a layer, layer styles provide a simple way to add an effect that is easy to edit and completely scalable—and can be re-used in other documents with one click. In this example, I copied the Background layer and then used the Image>Canvas Size command to add extra canvas to the document. Since the copied Background layer (Layer 1, in my example) has transparency around it, I can add layer styles. I clicked on the Add a Layer Style icon at the bottom of the Layers palette and chose Drop Shadow from the pop-up menu.

The changes you make in the Layer Style dialog will be immediately visible on the current layer. You can even position your cursor on the image and visually drag the effect into position, as I did here with the drop shadow. I also changed the Spread and Size of the shadow in the Structure section of the dialog.

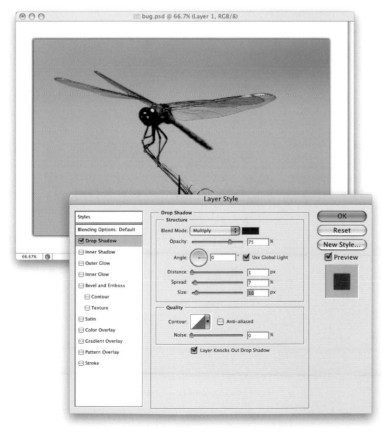

29

In this example, I also added Stroke and Inner Glow layer styles.

In the Layers palette, by clicking on the down-facing triangle to the right of the Layer Style icon, you can expand the view to see a list of the current layer styles applied. Then you can hide one or more effects by clicking on the Eye icon to the left of the layer style.

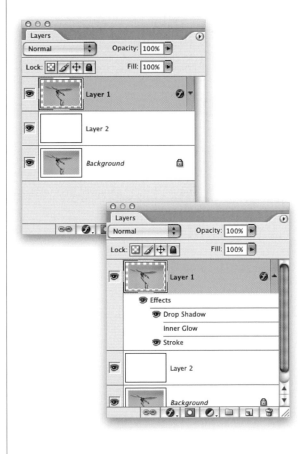

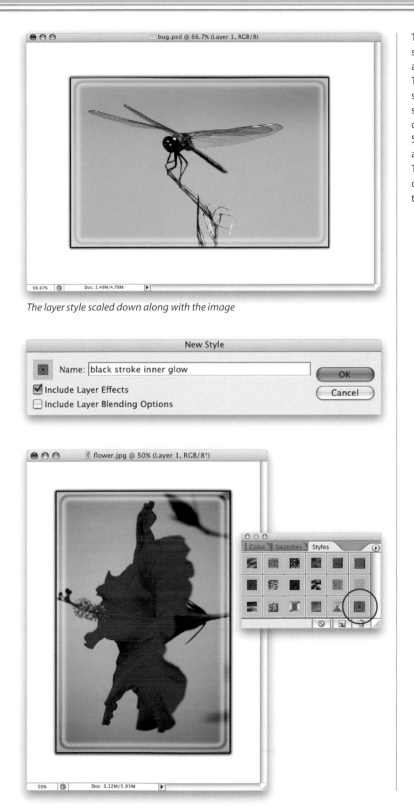

The layer style scaled down along with the image

There are two other great reasons to use layer styles. First, they are completely scalable, as shown in this example where I used Free Transform to scale down the layer and the layer styles changed with the layer. Second, you can save the layer style in the Styles palette for use on other layers. Just click on the Create New Style icon at the bottom of the Styles palette and name the style in the resulting dialog. Then make a layer active (in this example, in a completely different document) and click on the style to apply it to the layer.

threshold

What Makes a Good Threshold Image

One of the techniques that we'll use a number of times in the book is to convert a photo into a black-and-white pattern using a command called Threshold. Then we'll use the resulting image in a layer mask, as a pattern, and as a border itself. The question is, what kind of image works best for these techniques? And the answer, as it often is in Photoshop, is "it depends." It depends on what kind of effect you're looking for and how subtle or dramatic you want the end result to be. The results you get will vary with the image you're starting with, so let's take a look at a few examples that hopefully will help you look at your photos in a new light (especially photographs that you might otherwise throw away).

In most cases, you don't want to end up with an image that has too much white in it, nor do you want large areas of black. The simplest thing to do is to take a look at it while you move the slider in the Threshold dialog and see what you get.

Here's an example of a photo that I was ready to delete when I looked at it—one of those "missed it by that much" pictures where I almost got the shot I was looking for, but the bird flew a little faster than I wanted.

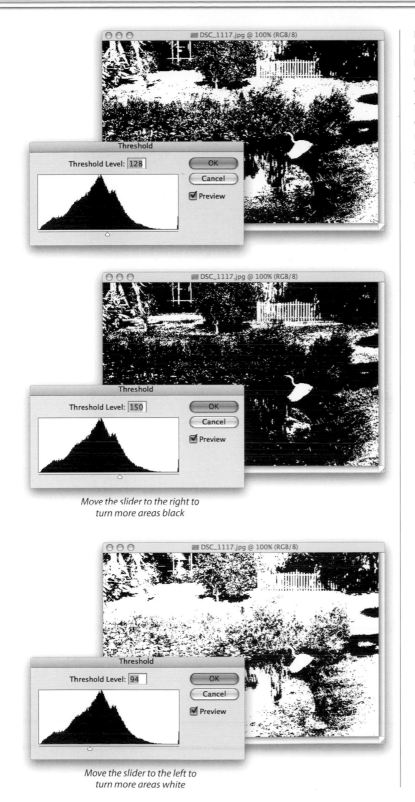

Move the slider to the right to
turn more areas black

Move the slider to the left to
turn more areas white

Remember, layer masks make use of black to hide areas of the layer, so converting a photo like this one to black-and-white shapes can create some interesting mask effects. From the Image menu, choose Adjustments> Threshold and take a look at the effect it has on the photo: all color and shades disappear, replaced with either black or white. Move the slider to the right and more areas will turn black; drag the slider to the left to make more areas turn white.

Another option is to take a look at a specific area of a photo to see what kind of border mask you can create. To do this, make a selection of a portion of the photo, and then add a Threshold adjustment layer. To look at various parts of the image, click on the Link icon between the layer and layer mask to unlink them. Then, with the layer mask active, use the Move tool to reposition the mask and look at different areas of the photo.

Once you find the area you want to use as a border, press-and-hold the Command key (PC: Control key) and click on the layer mask thumbnail to load the selection. Then, from the Edit menu, choose Copy Merged (to make a copy with the Threshold adjustment applied to the photo without having to flatten the document). Then you can switch to a different document and paste it onto an image or a layer mask (as we'll see later in the first such technique).

Ultimately, you may find yourself actually looking for things to shoot that you can turn into a great Threshold border. The following pages show two examples that I shot specifically to try as Threshold borders.

This first example is a picture I would never have taken in the past: it's not very interesting; it's a little busy; it's not a great photo for typical use in Photoshop. However, it occurred to me that the lines of the weeds might make an interesting image after applying Threshold, and they certainly did. The result contains nice angular lines that would provide some interesting effects as a border or used in a brush.

Here again is something I wouldn't even have glanced at before: the parking lot outside our office. But in the "that might make a great Threshold image" frame of mind, I started looking at things a little differently and shot this close-up of broken asphalt. Sure enough, the Threshold command turned the boring parking lot into a very interesting pattern that I can use in many different ways. Even if you're not sure how well the Threshold command will work on an image, why not take the shot and try using Threshold? You've got nothing to lose, and the potential for some very cool borders and patterns to gain.

II

frames & border effects

So this is where the fun begins, where we start sawing, gluing, and constructing our first frames. Wait, we were kinda going for the whole cooking theme, weren't we? All right, so this is where we start blending our ingredients together to bake ourselves a culinary masterpiece. Hmm, this is harder than I thought it would be, the whole "mix Photoshop with cooking metaphors" thing.

Let's try this again. This section contains a series of techniques to whet your appetite for tasty photographic delights, including frames, borders, edge effects, and more. Try out these step-by-step recipes and then go from there and see what appetizing creations you can cook up. Okay, I'm sorry, this just isn't working for me, so let's cut to the chase: jump in anywhere, try the steps shown, experiment, play, create, and enjoy. 'Nuff said.

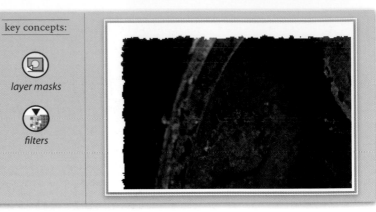

applying a filter to a layer mask

In this first technique, we'll go over some of the key steps that will be involved in many of the other techniques. Subsequent techniques will include these steps but I won't explain the "whys" in any great detail, since they build on these key functions.

key concepts:

layer masks

filters

Step One:

Press Command-J (PC: Control-J) to duplicate the Background layer. Although this is not a necessary step when you use layer masks, it does provide us with a backup plan since we're working on a copy of the photo (within the same document).

Step Two:

From the Image menu, choose Canvas Size (or press Command-Option-C [PC: Control-Alt-C]). In the Canvas Size dialog, make sure the Relative checkbox is turned on and enter 1 inch in both the Width and Height fields. It is important to duplicate the Background layer first and then add the extra canvas. This way the copied layer is the image surrounded by transparency.

Canvas Size

Current Size: 571.6K
Width: 7.528 inches
Height: 5 inches

New Size: 777.1K
Width: 1 inches
Height: 1 inches
☑ Relative
Anchor:

Canvas extension color: Background

OK
Cancel

TECHNIQUE #1

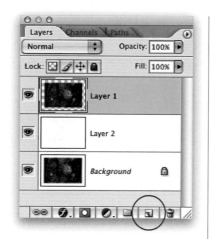

Step Three:

Press-and-hold the Command key (PC: Control key) and click on the Create a New Layer icon at the bottom of the Layers palette. This will create a new layer below the current layer, which saves you from having to create a layer and then drag it down in the layer stack. Press D to set your Foreground and Background to the default colors, and then press Command-Delete (PC: Control-Backspace) to fill the layer with white. We add a white layer so the effects of the layer mask are visible. Otherwise, areas of the copied layer would be hidden, causing the original to show through, resulting in no effect. If it sounds confusing, try hiding the white layer (by clicking on the Eye icon to the left of the layer thumbnail) after Step Five or Six and you'll see what I mean.

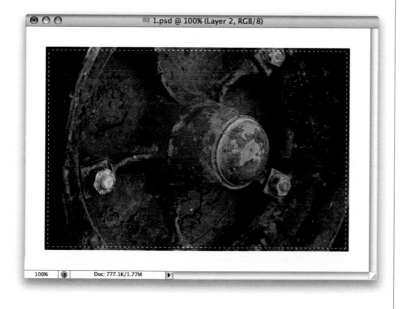

Step Four:

Press-and-hold the Command key (PC: Control key) and click on the top layer's thumbnail (the copied Background layer) to load it as a selection. From the Select menu, choose Modify>Contract and enter 5 pixels as the Contract By amount (for higher resolution images, try 10–15 pixels).

Step Five:

Make sure that the top layer is active and click on the Add Layer Mask icon at the bottom of the Layers palette. This will create a layer mask from your selection, which will result in a small portion of the top layer being hidden.

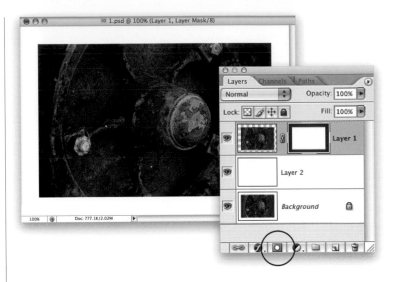

Step Six:

The layer mask should automatically be active, but if it isn't, click on the layer mask thumbnail. (A small black border around the four corners of the thumbnail indicates that it is active.) From the Filter menu, choose Brush Strokes>Spatter and experiment with the values to see the results you get. A lower value in the Spray Radius will give a subtle effect, while a high value will result in a "wilder" effect. In my example, I used a Spray Radius of 4 and a Smoothness value of 5. Here's the result.

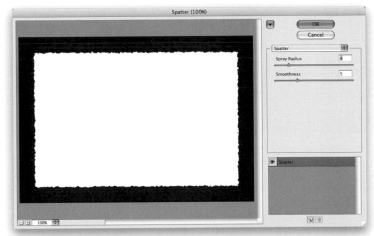

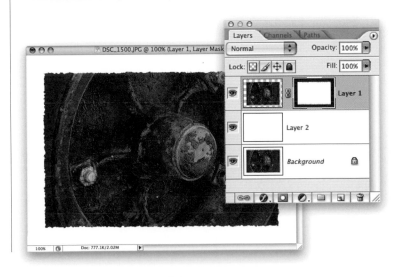

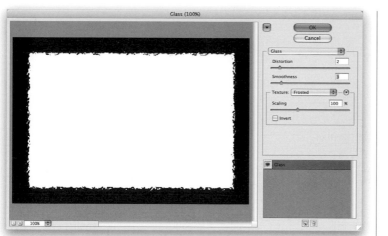

Needless to say, you can try any number of different filters, or several filters applied on top of each other. Here are a couple of examples that build on the Spatter filter:

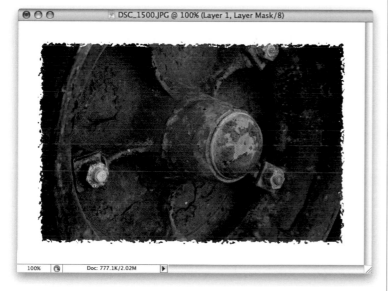

Here I applied the Glass filter (Filter>Distort>Glass).

In this example, I applied the Conté Crayon filter (Filter>Sketch>Conté Crayon), which introduces a bit of texture into the photo itself.

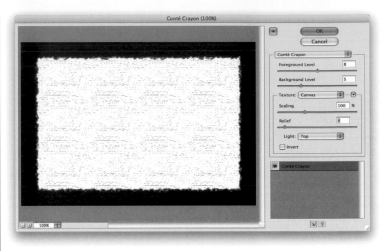

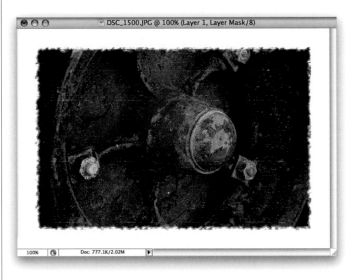

NOTE

The 1" of extra canvas added in Step Two was to give us room to experiment with the filters. Once you're finished with your experimentations, you can use Image>Trim to remove most of the extra canvas.

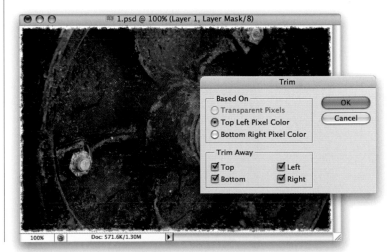

key concepts:

layer masks

filters

displacement mapping to a layer mask

Here's a variation on applying one of the typical filters, courtesy of photographer and Photoshop educator Eddie Tapp. Eddie shared his technique with me at Photoshop World, and with his permission I've included my slightly adapted version here. The key is using the Displace filter and some of the textures that are built into Photoshop.

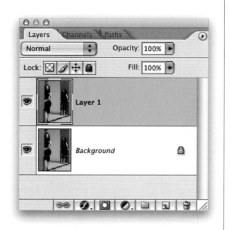

Step One:

Press Command-J (PC: Control-J) to duplicate the Background layer.

Step Two:

From the Image menu, choose Canvas Size (or press Command-Option-C [PC: Control-Alt-C]). In the Canvas Size dialog, make sure the Relative checkbox is turned on and enter 1 inch in both the Width and Height fields.

45

Step Three:

Press-and-hold the Command key (PC: Control key) and click on the Create a New Layer icon at the bottom of the Layers palette to create a new layer below the current layer. Press D to set your Foreground and Background to the default colors. Then press Command-Delete (PC: Control-Backspace) to fill the new layer with white.

Step Four:

Press-and-hold the Command key (PC: Control key) and click on the top layer's thumbnail (the copied Background layer) to load it as a selection. Make sure that the top layer is active and click on the Add Layer Mask icon at the bottom of the Layers palette to create a layer mask from your selection.

Step Five:

With the layer mask selected, from the Filter menu, choose Distort>Displace. This filter needs lots of experimentation, but to start off, in the Displace dialog, try using numbers from 10–20 for Horizontal and Vertical Scale. Click OK, then in the resulting Open dialog, you'll choose the displacement map to use with the filter. You can find a series of built-in textures that you can use as a displacement map on a Mac in Hard Drive:Applications:Adobe Photoshop CS2:Presets:Textures, or in Windows in C:\Program Files\Adobe\Adobe Photoshop CS2\Presets\Textures. In this example, I used the Frosted Glass texture.

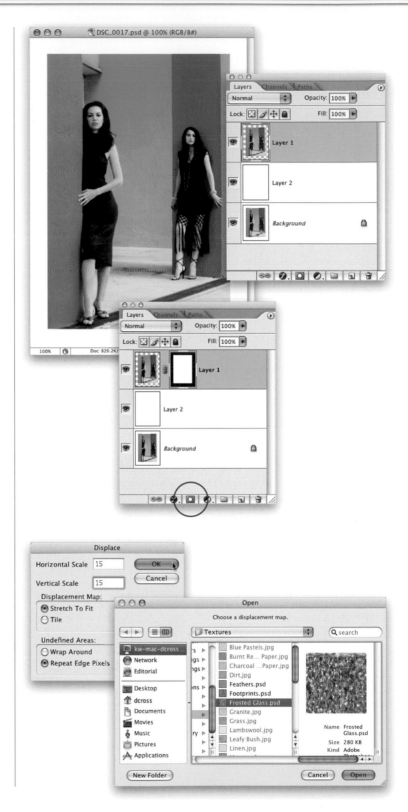

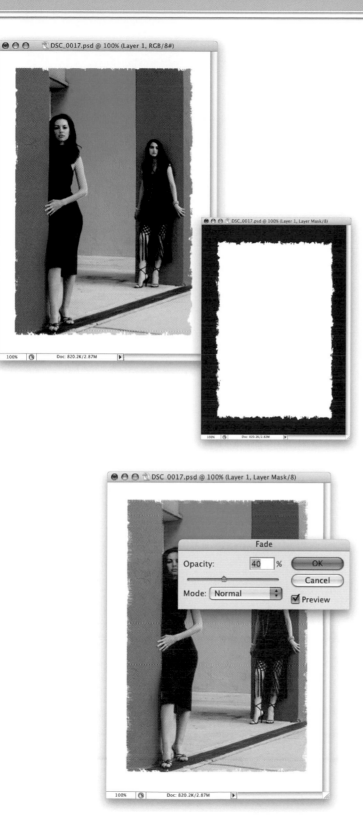

As a result, the layer mask looks like the capture you see here.

TIP

The goodies CD that ships with Photoshop includes additional textures that you can load and use as displacement maps.

Step Six:

You can also get some interesting effects by applying the Displace filter again using different settings and a different displacement map, and then using the Fade command. Here I chose Lines as the displacement map, then chose Edit>Fade Displace, and then lowered the Opacity to 40%.

variations:

Here's the result of using the Fade command with the Opacity set to 60% and Mode set to Hard Light.

Variation 1: Fade with Hard Light blend mode

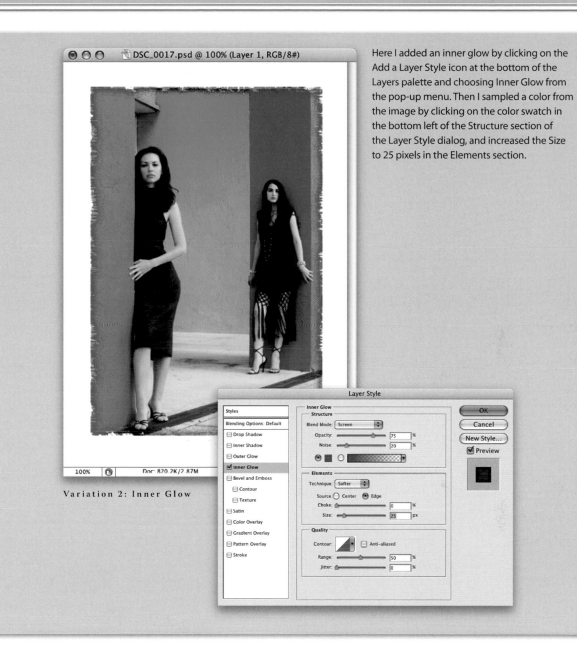

Here I added an inner glow by clicking on the Add a Layer Style icon at the bottom of the Layers palette and choosing Inner Glow from the pop-up menu. Then I sampled a color from the image by clicking on the color swatch in the bottom left of the Structure section of the Layer Style dialog, and increased the Size to 25 pixels in the Elements section.

Variation 2: Inner Glow

In this example, using the Elliptical Marquee tool (press Shift-M until it comes up), I created a feathered selection, and then created a layer mask from the selection. I then applied the Displace filter using the Frosted Glass texture.

Variation 3: Displace filter

key concepts:

layer masks

define brush

dry brush painting on a layer mask

While the first two techniques rely on the effects of a filter, this time around you will have a much greater influence on the result by painting on the layer mask. The first few steps in this technique are the same as in the previous techniques, so I'll go through them pretty quickly without explaining each step.

Step One:

Press Command-J (PC: Control-J) to duplicate the Background layer.

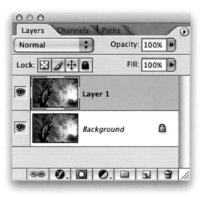

Step Two:

From the Image menu, choose Canvas Size (or press Command-Option-C [PC: Control-Alt-C]). In the Canvas Size dialog, make sure the Relative checkbox is turned on and enter 1 inch in both the Width and Height fields.

Step Three:

Press-and-hold the Command key (PC: Control key) and click on the Create a New Layer icon at the bottom of the Layers palette to create a layer below the current layer. Press D to set your Foreground and Background to the default colors. Then press Command-Delete (PC: Control-Backspace) to fill the new layer with white.

Step Four:

Press-and-hold the Command key (PC: Control key) and click on the top layer's thumbnail (the copied Background layer) to load it as a selection. From the Select menu, choose Modify>Contract, enter 2 pixels as the Contract By amount, and click OK (for higher resolution images try 5–10 pixels).

Step Five:

Make sure that the top layer is active and click on the Add Layer Mask icon at the bottom of the Layers palette to create a layer mask from your selection.

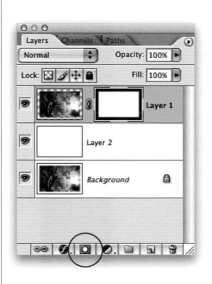

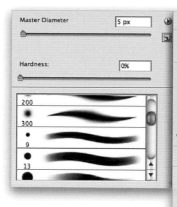

Step Six:

From the Toolbox, choose the Brush tool (B), and then in the Options Bar, click on the Brush thumbnail. In the resulting Brush Picker, click on the right-facing triangle and choose Dry Media Brushes from the flyout menu. Go ahead and click OK in the resulting dialog and replace your current brushes—you can always choose Reset Brushes from the same flyout menu to get back to the default set. Choose one of the Dry Media brushes. I chose Pastel Medium Tip for this example.

Step Seven:

Make sure the layer mask is still active and click once on the top-right corner of the photo. Press-and-hold the Shift key, move to the top-left corner of the photo, and click again. The Brush tool will paint a straight line between your two clicks.

Step Eight:

Repeat this operation for all four sides of the photo, and don't worry about trying to stay perfectly horizontal or vertical. In fact, you can add to the randomness of the effect by deliberately painting slightly askew. Here's the result, along with a view of the layer mask.

Of course, each brush will have a different effect and you shouldn't restrict yourself to just the Dry Media brushes. You can try any of the built-in brushes or, as we'll see in the next technique, make your own.

Here's another example where I chose a smaller brush, changed the Foreground color to white, and lowered the Brush tool's opacity (in the Options Bar) to around 60%.

making your own brush

This technique involves painting on a layer mask, but using a brush that you define from the image itself. As with the previous techniques, this one starts the same way: creating a layer mask on a copy of the Background layer.

key concepts:

layer masks

define brush

Step One:

Press Command-J (PC: Control-J) to duplicate the Background layer.

Step Two:

From the Image menu, choose Canvas Size (or press Command-Option-C [PC: Control-Alt-C]). In the Canvas Size dialog, make sure the Relative checkbox is turned on and enter 1 inch in both the Width and Height fields.

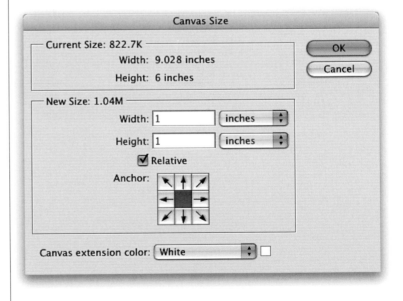

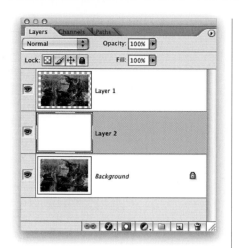

Step Three:

Press-and-hold the Command key (PC: Control key) and click on the Create a New Layer icon at the bottom of the Layers palette to create a new layer below the current layer. Press D to set your Foreground and Background to the default colors. Then press Command-Delete (PC: Control-Backspace) to fill the new layer with white.

Step Four:

This time around, we'll make a selection by choosing the Rectangular Marquee tool (M) and clicking-and-dragging to create a selection that leaves a small border (rather than using Modify>Contract like we did previously).

Step Five:

Make sure that the top layer is active and click on the Add Layer Mask icon at the bottom of the Layers palette to create a layer mask from your selection.

Step Six:

Again, using the Rectangular Marquee tool, select an area of the photo that spans the width of the entire image. You can experiment with the height of the selection and add a feathered edge if you want. (In my example, there's no feathering on the selection.)

Step Seven:

In the Layers palette, click on the Background layer to activate it, and then from the Edit menu, choose Define Brush Preset. Name your new brush and click OK. Press Command-D (PC: Control-D) to Deselect.

TIP

Once you've defined some custom brushes, it's a good idea to create a backup version so you don't lose these brushes. To do this, use Edit>Preset Manager and choose Brushes from the Preset Type pop-up menu. While pressing-and-holding the Command key (PC: Control key), click on each of your custom brushes until you have them all selected. Then click Save Set and, in the Save dialog, save your brushes in a safe place. If you want your brush set to automatically appear in the Brushes palette, save your brushes in Hard Drive:Applications:Adobe Photoshop CS2:Presets:Brushes on a Mac or in C:\Program Files\Adobe\Adobe Photoshop CS2\Presets\Brushes in Windows.

Step Eight:

In the Layers palette, click on the layer mask to select it and press D to set the Foreground color to black. Select the Brush tool (B) and in the Options Bar, click on the Brush thumbnail. In the resulting Brush Picker, choose your new brush (it will be at the very bottom of the list), and position the brush on the edge of your photo. Click once to paint with your custom brush.

NOTE
If you want to use the brush more than once on the same side of your photo, just reposition it slightly.

Step Nine:

Repeat Steps Six and Seven, but this time with a vertical selection to create a brush that you'll use for the left and right sides of the layer mask.

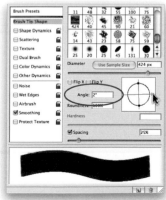

Hint: Using the Brushes palette (docked in the Palette Well), you can slightly angle the brush by entering a value in the Angle field (I suggest a very slight angle, something in the 1–3° range).

Here's the final result with a view of the layer mask.

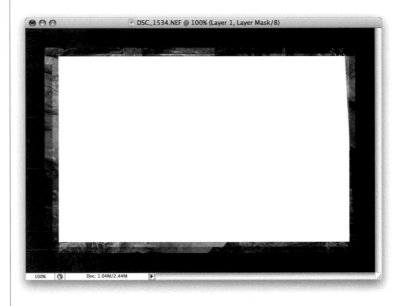

TECHNIQUE #4

variations:

In this variation, I applied the Spatter filter (Filter>Brush Strokes>Spatter) to the layer mask.

Variation 1: Spatter filter

Variation 2: Sampled color

Here I sampled a color from the photo and filled the (formerly white) layer below the layer mask layer with the sampled color. To do this, simply click on your Foreground color swatch to open the Color Picker, then click your cursor on the color in your image you want to sample and click OK. Click on the white layer and press Option-Delete (PC: Alt-Backspace) to fill it with your new Foreground color.

TECHNIQUE #5

making your own brush with a pattern

In this slight variation of the previous technique, we'll once again paint on a layer mask using a brush. This time the brush will paint using a pattern as a texture rather than as a brush shape. Again, the first few steps are the same as in the previous techniques.

key concepts:

layer masks

quick mask

define pattern

define brush

Step One:

Press Command-J (PC: Control-J) to duplicate the Background layer.

Step Two:

From the Image menu, choose Canvas Size (or press Command-Option-C [PC: Control-Alt-C]). In the Canvas Size dialog, make sure the Relative checkbox is turned on and enter 1 inch in both the Width and Height fields.

TECHNIQUE #5

Step Three:

Press-and-hold the Command key (PC: Control key) and click on the Create a New Layer icon at the bottom of the Layers palette to create a new layer below the current layer. Press D to set your Foreground and Background to the default colors. Then press Command-Delete (PC: Control-Backspace) to fill the new layer with white.

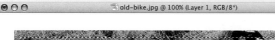

Step Four:

As in the previous technique, we'll make a selection by choosing the Rectangular Marquee tool (M) and clicking-and-dragging to create a selection that leaves a small border (rather than using Modify>Contract like we did earlier).

Step Five:

Make sure that the top layer is active and click on the Add Layer Mask icon at the bottom of the Layers palette to create a layer mask from your selection.

Step Six:

Again, using the Rectangular Marquee tool, select an area of the photo that spans the width of the entire image. (To show the selection in Quick Mask mode, I pressed the letter Q. If you do use Quick Mask mode to view your selection, you'll have to return to Standard mode before the next step. Just press Q again.)

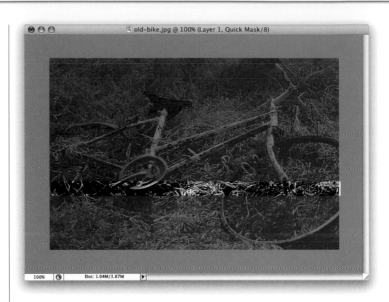

Step Seven:

In the Layers palette, click on the Background layer to activate it, and then from the Edit menu, choose Define Pattern. Name your new pattern and click OK.

Step Eight:

Choose the Brush tool (B) and start with a basic brush. (If you need to reset your brushes to the default, go to the Brush Picker's flyout menu and choose Reset Brushes.) Once you have chosen and resized your brush, go to the Brush Picker's flyout menu, and choose New Brush Preset. Name your new brush, click OK, and then press Command-D (PC: Control-D) to Deselect. (We do this so we don't change the settings of one of the built-in brushes.)

Step Nine:

From the Palette Well, open the Brushes palette and click on the Texture option. At the top of the palette, click on the Pattern thumbnail and from the resulting Pattern Picker, select the pattern you just defined. Experiment with the blend mode to determine how the brush and texture interact. In this example, I chose Hard Mix from the Mode pop-up menu (take advantage of the preview area at the bottom of the palette to see what your settings will create).

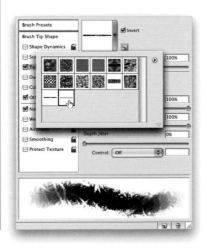

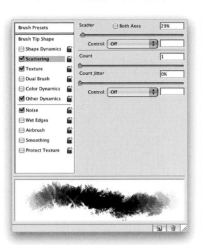

If you want, you can also try other settings to see the effect it has on your brush. Here, I chose Scattering and adjusted the settings.

Step Ten:

With the layer mask active and black as your Foreground color, click once on the top left of the image. Press-and-hold the Shift key and move your mouse over and click once on the top-right corner of the Image. Repeat for the bottom of the image. Rather than using the same brush for the sides, we'll define a new vertical pattern (if you did use the same brush to paint vertically, you'd get a very noticeable repeating pattern).

Step Eleven:

Repeat Steps Six and Seven to make a pattern, this time selecting a vertical portion of the image. Again, make sure you've clicked on the Background layer before using Edit>Define Pattern. Then go back to the Brushes palette and choose the new vertical pattern.

Here's the result, including a view of the layer mask.

Variation 1: Plastic Wrap filter

variation:

Here I applied the Plastic Wrap filter to the layer mask that I had just painted.

painting along a layer mask's path

Here's another variation on painting the edges of a layer mask—automatic painting, thanks to a path. As before, we'll create a copy of the image and add a layer mask, but then we'll create and use a path to do the work for us.

key concepts:

layer masks

define brush

Step One:

Press Command-J (PC: Control-J) to duplicate the Background layer.

Step Two:

From the Image menu, choose Canvas Size (or press Command-Option-C [PC: Control-Alt-C]). In the Canvas Size dialog, make sure the Relative checkbox is turned on and enter 1 inch in both the Width and Height fields.

Canvas Size

Current Size: 607.2K
Width: 5.292 inches
Height: 7.556 inches

New Size: 817.5K
Width: 1 — inches
Height: 1 — inches
☑ Relative
Anchor:

Canvas extension color: White

OK
Cancel

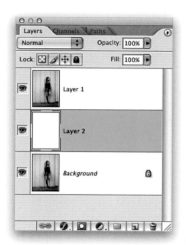

Step Three:

Press-and-hold the Command key (PC: Control key) and click on the Create a New Layer icon at the bottom of the Layers palette to create a new layer below the current layer. Press D to set your Foreground and Background to the default colors. Then press Command-Delete (PC: Control-Backspace) to fill the new layer with white.

Step Four:

As in the previous technique, we'll make a selection by choosing the Rectangular Marquee tool (M) and clicking-and-dragging to create a selection that leaves a small border (rather than using Modify>Contract).

Step Five:

Make sure that the top layer is active and click on the Add Layer Mask icon at the bottom of the Layers palette to create a layer mask from your selection.

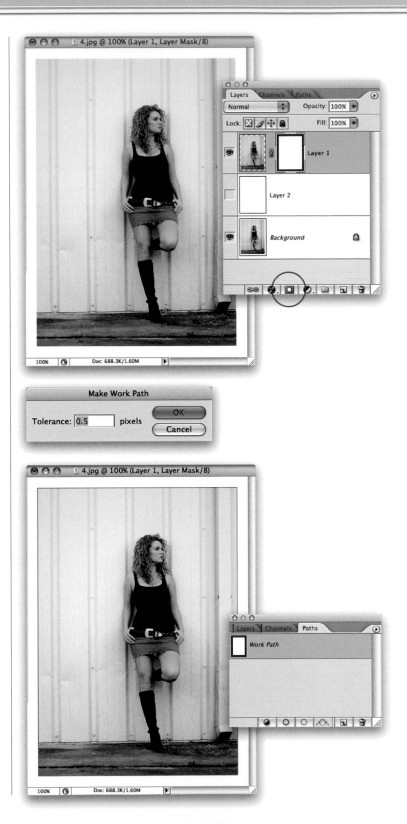

Step Six:

Press-and-hold the Command key (PC: Control key) and click on the layer mask thumbnail to make a selection the same size as the mask. Then, switch to the Paths palette (nested behind the Layers palette by default) and from the palette's flyout menu, choose Make Work Path. In the resulting dialog, enter a Tolerance of 0.5 pixels (the lowest number possible, creating a more accurate path).

A path will now be visible around the edges of the photo. This path is a non-printing element that is used for various purposes such as making a selection, or as we'll use it here, to apply a stroke.

Step Seven:

Choose the Brush tool (B) and in the Options Bar enter the settings you want to use—particularly choosing the brush and setting the opacity. As in all the exercises, you can experiment with many different settings here. *Note:* Make sure your Foreground color is set to black by pressing D.

Step Eight:

In the Layers palette, make sure that the layer mask is active, and then switch back to the Paths palette. Make sure the path is active (indicated by the fact that the Work Path is highlighted in the palette), press-and-hold the Option key (PC: Alt key), and click on the Stroke Path with Brush icon at the bottom of the palette (the second icon from the left). In the Stroke Path dialog, make sure Brush is selected in the Tool pop-up menu. Here's the result based upon the brush and opacity settings I chose in Step Seven.

TECHNIQUE #6

variation:

Another option is to turn on the Simulate Pressure checkbox in the Stroke Path dialog. Here's an example, created by using a different brush and simulating pressure.

Variation 1: Simulate Pressure

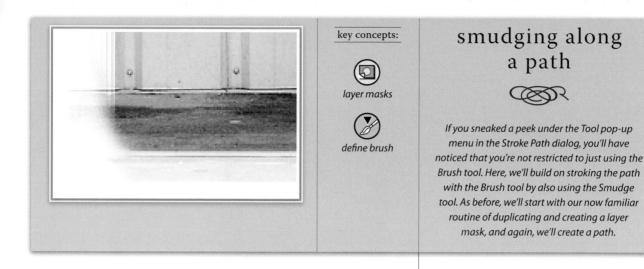

key concepts:

layer masks

define brush

smudging along a path

If you sneaked a peek under the Tool pop-up menu in the Stroke Path dialog, you'll have noticed that you're not restricted to just using the Brush tool. Here, we'll build on stroking the path with the Brush tool by also using the Smudge tool. As before, we'll start with our now familiar routine of duplicating and creating a layer mask, and again, we'll create a path.

Step One:

Press Command-J (PC: Control-J) to duplicate the Background layer.

Step Two:

From the Image menu, choose Canvas Size (or press Command-Option-C [PC: Control-Alt-C]). In the Canvas Size dialog, make sure the Relative checkbox is turned on and enter 1 inch in both the Width and Height fields.

73

Step Three:

Press-and-hold the Command key (PC: Control key) and click on the Create a New Layer icon at the bottom of the Layers palette to create a new layer below the current layer. Press D to set your Foreground and Background to the default colors. Then press Command-Delete (PC: Control-Backspace) to fill the new layer with white.

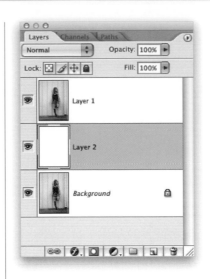

Step Four:

Make a selection inside the edge of your image by choosing the Rectangular Marquee tool (M) and clicking-and-dragging to create a selection that leaves a small border.

Step Five:

Make sure that the top layer is active and click on the Add Layer Mask icon at the bottom of the Layers palette to create a layer mask from your selection.

Step Six:

Press-and-hold the Command key (PC: Control key) and click on the layer mask thumbnail to make a selection the same size as the mask. Then, from the Paths palette's flyout menu, choose Make Work Path. In the resulting dialog, enter a Tolerance of 0.5 pixels.

Step Seven:

Choose the Brush tool (B) and in the Options Bar enter the settings you want to use—particularly choosing the brush and setting the opacity. (*Note:* Make sure your Foreground color is set to black by pressing D.) In the Layers palette, make sure that the layer mask is active, and then switch back to the Paths palette. Make sure the path is active (indicated by the fact that the Work Path is highlighted in the palette), press-and-hold the Option key (PC: Alt key), and click on the Stroke Path with Brush icon at the bottom of the palette (the second icon from the left). In the Stroke Path dialog, make sure Brush is selected in the Tool pop-up menu.

Step Eight:

Now choose the Smudge tool (R) and in the Options Bar, enter the settings you want to use, particularly choosing the brush and setting the strength—try using a strength higher than the default.

Step Nine:

Again, make sure that the layer mask is active, and then switch back to the Paths palette. Make sure the path is active, press-and-hold the Option key (PC: Alt key), and click on the Stroke Path with Brush icon at the bottom of the palette. From the Stroke Path dialog, choose Smudge from the Tool pop-up menu, if it's not already selected, and turn on the Simulate Pressure checkbox. Here's the result based upon the brush and opacity settings I chose.

Here's the result, along with the layer mask, after I repeated the smudge effect with a larger brush.

variation:

Here I added a Drop Shadow layer style with a color I sampled from the bottom of the image.

Variation 1: Color drop shadow

key concepts:

filters

layer masks

extracting a border

When I showed this technique on Adobe® Photoshop® TV *my cohosts laughed at my description of this as an "adventurous" technique. So maybe it would better be described as unpredictable, since the results you get will vary dramatically depending on your photo and the highlight you create in the Extract filter. Still, it offers some interesting possibilities.*

Step One:

Press Command-J (PC: Control-J) to duplicate the Background layer. Press-and-hold the Command key (PC: Control key) and click on the Create a New Layer icon at the bottom of the Layers palette to add a new layer below the copied Background layer. Press D to set your Foreground and Background to the default colors, and then press Command-Delete (PC: Control-Backspace) to fill the new layer with white.

Step Two:

Click on the copied Background layer and from the Filter menu, choose Extract. With the Edge Highlighter tool (B), choose a small brush size and click once just inside the top-left corner of the photo. Press-and-hold the Shift key and click on the top-right corner of the photo. Continue painting straight lines to create a border, each time leaving a small amount of space between your painted border and the edge of the photo. For a more unusual border, paint some additional short lines here and there, and press-and-hold the Option key (PC: Alt key) while you paint to remove some areas of the border. (You can also paint a highlighted border freehand if you like—just make sure there are no gaps in the border as I mention in the next step.)

79

Step Three:

Using the Fill tool (G), click once inside the border to fill the inside area with blue. If the blue fill spills outside the border, press Command-Z (PC: Control-Z) to Undo and use the Edge Highlighter tool to close up any gaps. Then click OK.

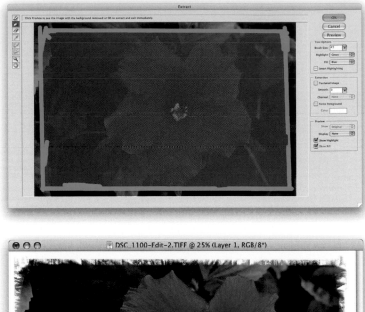

The result, or should I say the unpredictable result, will depend on the colors in your image and the width of the border you highlighted, but in general this should give you a pretty interesting effect. Of course, you could continue to work with this border effect, especially if you turn it into a layer mask as shown in these next few steps.

Step Four:

Click on the original Background layer and press Command-J (PC: Control-J) to duplicate it. Drag the Background copy layer above the white layer.

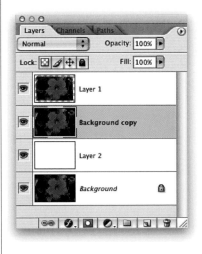

Step Five:

Press-and-hold the Command key (PC: Control key) and click on the extracted layer's thumbnail to create a selection that follows the extracted border. Click on the Eye icon beside the extracted layer to hide it, and make sure the Background copy layer you made in Step Four is active.

Step Six:

Click on the Add Layer Mask icon at the bottom of the Layers palette to create a layer mask for your Background copy layer, which will duplicate the results of the Extract filter. By creating a layer mask, you can experiment further by applying filters or using a custom brush to tweak the mask.

variations:

Here, I applied the Dry Brush filter to the layer mask to alter the effect slightly.

Variation 1: Dry Brush filter

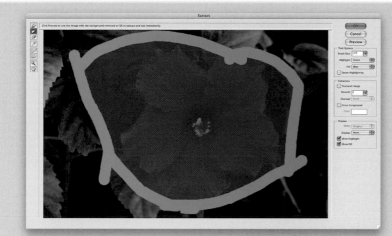

In this case, I painted a series of random lines with the Edge Highlighter tool (making sure to create a closed outline), and then made a layer mask as previously described. I applied a slight Gaussian Blur to the mask, and then lowered the opacity of the white layer so that the original background showed through slightly.

Variation 2

83

TECHNIQUE #9

extracting a border and burning the edges

In this variation, we'll use the Extract filter to create a border and then add a color effect to the edges of the resulting border.

key concepts:

filters

blend modes

Step One:

Press Command-J (PC: Control-J) to duplicate the Background layer. Press-and-hold the Command key (PC: Control key) and click on the Create a New Layer icon at the bottom of the Layers palette to add a new layer below the copied Background layer. Press D to set your Foreground and Background to the default colors, and then press Command-Delete (PC: Control-Backspace) to fill the new layer with white.

TECHNIQUE #9

Step Two:

Click on the copied Background layer and from the Filter menu choose Extract. Using the Edge Highlighter tool (B) with the Shift key held down, click once in each corner of the photo to create a border, each time leaving a small amount of space between your painted border and the edge of the photo. Using the Fill tool (G), click once inside the border to fill the inside area with blue. Then, click OK.

Here's the result I got in this case.

Step Three:

Press-and-hold the Command key (PC: Control key) and click on the thumbnail of the extracted layer to load it as a selection, and then press Command-Shift-I (PC: Control-Shift-I) to Inverse the selection.

Step Four:

Add a new layer on top of the layer stack by making your top layer active and clicking on the Create a New Layer icon. Then, click on your Foreground color swatch at the bottom of the Toolbox and choose a color in the Color Picker—a bright orange shade is a good starting place, but of course any color you choose will produce a different effect. Press Option-Delete (PC: Alt-Backspace) to fill the selection on the new layer with your color. Press Command-D (PC: Control-D) to Deselect.

Step Five:

Change the blend mode of the top layer (using the pop-up menu at the top of the Layers palette) from Normal to Color Burn, and the color will only appear on the edges of the extracted border.

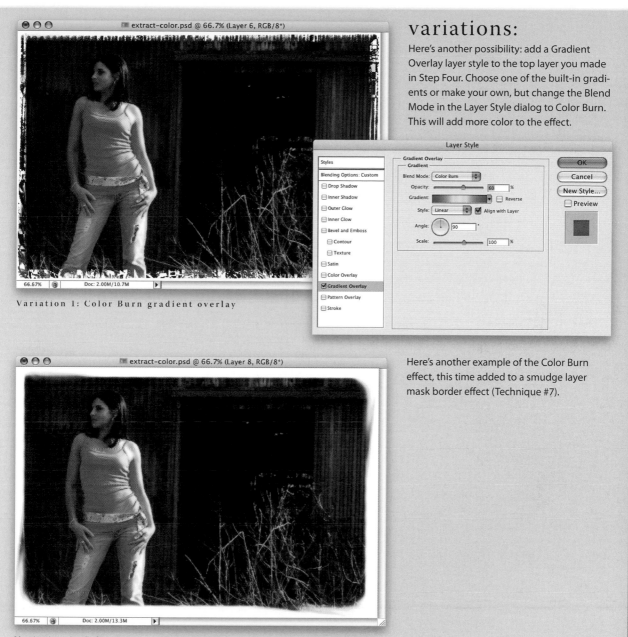

Variation 1: Color Burn gradient overlay

Variation 2: Color Burn with smudge layer mask

variations:

Here's another possibility: add a Gradient Overlay layer style to the top layer you made in Step Four. Choose one of the built-in gradients or make your own, but change the Blend Mode in the Layer Style dialog to Color Burn. This will add more color to the effect.

Here's another example of the Color Burn effect, this time added to a smudge layer mask border effect (Technique #7).

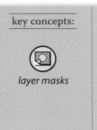

getting that painted-on look

key concepts:

layer masks

This technique lets us create the effect of a photo painted onto a canvas, and we'll achieve this in a very flexible way that can easily be edited.

Step One:

Press-and-hold the Option key (PC: Alt key) and double-click on the Background layer in the Layers palette (to unlock the layer so we can add a layer mask to it).

Step Two:

Press-and-hold the Option key (PC: Alt key) again, and click on the Add Layer Mask icon at the bottom of the Layers palette (this will add a layer mask filled with black, so all you will see at this point is the layer transparency checkerboard).

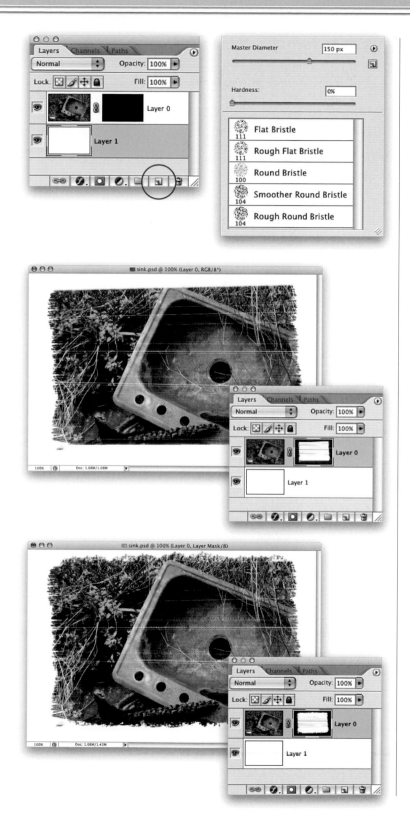

Step Three:

Now we'll add a new layer below our photo by pressing-and-holding the Command key (PC: Control key) and clicking on the Create a New Layer icon at the bottom of the Layers palette. Fill this new layer with white by pressing D to set your Foreground and Background to their default colors, and then pressing Command-Delete (PC: Control-Backspace).

Step Four:

With the Brush tool (B) selected, we need to change to some of the more unusual brushes. Click on the Brush thumbnail in the Options Bar and from the Brush Picker's flyout menu, choose Thick Heavy Brushes from the list of built-in brushes. Click OK to temporarily replace the default brushes (you can always choose Reset Brushes from the flyout menu to return to the default set).

Step Five:

Choose one of the new brushes in your Brush Picker, press X to set your Foreground color to white, click on the layer mask thumbnail in the Layers palette, and paint to reveal the original photo as shown here. Of course, you can experiment with different brush shapes, sizes, and opacities. In the second example, I painted the top and bottom edges with a different brush from the Thick Heavy Brushes set.

variation:

Here's another variation where I changed the underlying layer from white to black and applied the Texturizer filter (go to Filter>Texture>Texturizer, and choose Canvas from the Texture pop-up menu) to the layer mask.

Variation 1: Texturizer filter

key concepts:

illustrator to photoshop

layer masks

inserting a shape from illustrator

If you own Illustrator CS2, you have an extra tool that can easily be used to create interesting shape effects. (This assumes you know at least the basics of using Illustrator, of course.)

Step One:

Create a basic rectangle in Illustrator filled with black, and then add some extra paths, stroking them using some of the wonderful brush libraries, such as Artistic-Chalk Charcoal Pencil. Select everything (press Command-A [PC: Control-A] to Select All) and choose Edit>Copy, or press Command-C (PC: Control-C).

Step Two:

In your Photoshop document, press-and-hold the Option key (PC: Alt key) and double-click on the Background layer to unlock and rename it. Then, hold down the Command key (PC: Control key) and click on the Create a New Layer icon to add a new layer below the renamed Background layer. Press D to set your Foreground and Background colors to their defaults, and fill that layer with white by pressing Command-Delete (PC: Control-Backspace).

91

Step Three:

Press Command-V (PC: Control-V) to Paste the copied Illustrator artwork. In this example, we'll use the Paste As Pixels option to create a layer based on the copied Illustrator artwork.

Step Four:

If necessary, use the transformation handles to resize the pasted graphic (press-and-hold the Shift key and click on the corner handles to resize proportionally), and then press Return (PC: Enter) to finalize the size.

Step Five:

Drag the shape layer in between the white layer (Layer 1) and the photo layer (Layer 0). Click on the top layer (the photo layer) and then from the Layer menu choose Create Clipping Mask or press Command-Option-G (PC: Control-Alt-G). The photo layer will only be visible within the pixels of the shape layer immediately below it.

In order to edit the shape of your photo, you have to either add more pixels to the copied Illustrator layer where you want the photo to show, or erase pixels in areas where you don't want to see the image. To give yourself a little more flexibility, consider turning the shape into a layer mask.

If you've already pasted the shape from Illustrator and pressed Return to finalize the size, here's what you do to create a layer mask: press-and-hold the Command key (PC: Control key) and click on the thumbnail of the shape layer to make a selection in that shape. Click on the photo layer to activate it, and then click on the Add Layer Mask icon at the bottom of the Layers palette.

If you want to go directly from Illustrator to creating a layer mask, well, you can't. You'll have to paste the graphic, hit Return, and then follow the steps above to make a layer mask.

Creating a layer mask offers one big advantage over the clipping mask: you can apply filters to or paint on the layer mask to change the mask.

inserting a shape from illustrator as a smart object

Building on the last technique, this time we'll take advantage of the ability to insert a file as a Smart Object to create a live link between your Photoshop document and the Illustrator artwork. (The first few steps are identical to the last technique—you're not seeing double.)

key concepts:

illustrator to photoshop

Step One:

Create a basic rectangle in Illustrator filled with black, and then add some extra paths, stroking them with custom brushes. Select everything and choose Edit>Copy.

Step Two:

In your Photoshop document, press-and-hold the Option key (PC: Alt key) and double-click on the Background layer to unlock and rename it. Then, hold down the Command key (PC: Control key) and click on the Create a New Layer icon to add a new layer below the renamed Background layer. Press D to set your Foreground and Background colors to their defaults, and fill that layer with white by pressing Command-Delete (PC: Control-Backspace).

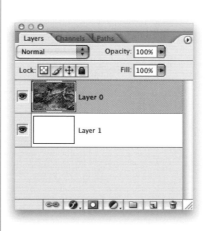

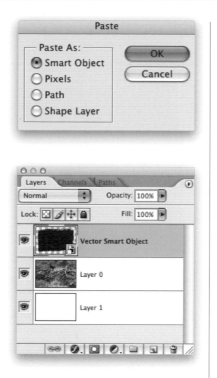

Step Three:

Press Command-V (PC: Control-V) to Paste the copied Illustrator artwork. In the Paste dialog, choose Paste As Smart Object.

Step Four:

If necessary, use the transformation handles to resize the pasted graphic (press-and-hold the Shift key and click on the corner handles to resize proportionally), and then press Return (PC: Enter) to finalize the size. You'll notice that the layer is labeled "Vector Smart Object."

Step Five:

Drag the shape layer in between the white layer (Layer 1) and the photo layer (Layer 0). Click on the top layer (the photo layer) and then from the Layer menu choose Create Clipping Mask or press Command-Option-G (PC: Control-Alt-G). The photo layer will only be visible within the pixels of the shape layer immediately below it.

Step Six:

To edit the original shape in Illustrator, just double-click on the Smart Object icon (the layer thumbnail). A new document called Vector Smart Object will open in Illustrator. Edit that shape, close the document, and save the changes.

Step Seven:

When you switch back to Photoshop, the Smart Object will update, and the clipping mask will affect the photo.

The only downside to using a Smart Object is you cannot paint on it or apply a filter to it—you have to do all your editing in Illustrator.

key concepts:

layer masks

free transform

scanning in a shape

If you still have access to a scanner, you can have some fun playing with this idea. Take a piece of paper or a white card and paint on it— I mean with real paint (or great big markers). Scan it in (after it's dry of course) and use that as a shape in a layer mask. (Hint: Scan it at a higher resolution than you think you'll need so you have some room to play with resizing.)

Here's the result of my scan.

Step One:

Take a look at your scan and see what you've got. If necessary, as it was in this case, use Curves to brighten up the area around your shape. Click on the Set White Point eyedropper icon at the bottom right of the Curves dialog, and then click with the eyedropper on a color in your image that's not as white as it should be (the background around your shape should be nice and white).

Step Two:

Press Command-A (PC: Control-A) to Select All, and then Command-C (PC: Control-C) to Copy.

Step Three:

Switch to your photo, and while holding down the Option key (PC: Alt key), double-click on the Background layer to rename it. Click on the Add Layer Mask icon at the bottom of the Layers palette to add a layer mask to the photo layer. Then, Command-click (PC: Control-click) on the Create a New Layer icon to add a new layer below your photo. Press D to set your Foreground and Background to their default colors, and press Command-Delete (PC: Control-Backspace) to fill it with white.

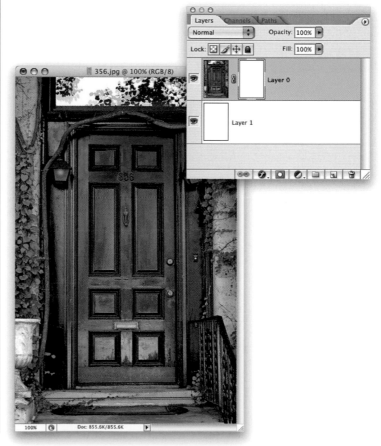

Step Four:

Press-and-hold the Option key (PC: Alt key) and click on the layer mask thumbnail to view the contents of the mask. Press Command-V (PC: Control-V) to Paste the scanned shape that you copied in Step Two. Don't deselect yet.

Step Five:

Press the Tilde key (~) to view the layer mask as a colored overlay, and then press Command-T (PC: Control-T) to bring up Free Transform. Use the handles to resize the graphic. (*Hint:* If you can't see the Free Transform handles, press Command-0 [PC: Control-0] to Fit on Screen—now you can see and work with the handles.) Press Return (PC: Enter) once you're done, then press Command-D (PC: Control-D) to Deselect.

Step Six:

Option-click (PC: Alt-click) on the layer thumbnail to view the results and you'll see the opposite of what you want: the area inside the shape is masked, rather than the other way around. Click on the layer mask thumbnail to activate the mask, and then press Command-I (PC: Control-I) to Invert the mask and get the result you want. (You could've also inverted the image back in Step Two before you copied it so that when it was pasted, the mask would be white on black. Then this step would be unnecessary.)

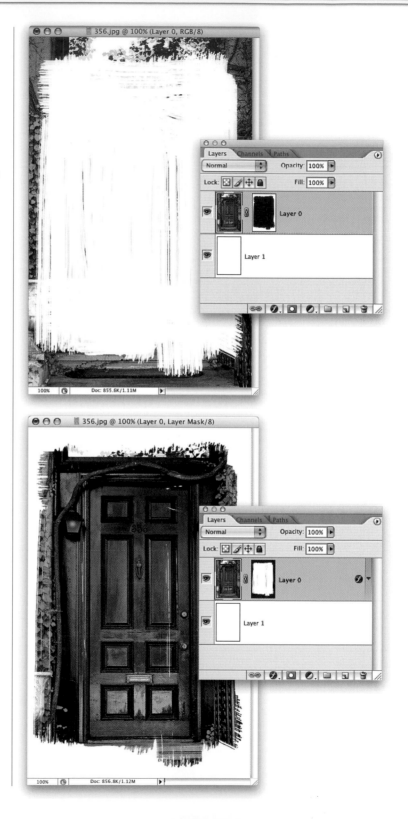

variations:

Try applying a filter to the layer mask. Here I clicked on the layer mask thumbnail and used Filter>Artistic>Rough Pastels.

Add a layer style to the layer. In the second example, I clicked on the Add a Layer Style icon and added a drop shadow and an inner shadow.

Variation 1: Rough Pastels filter

Variation 2: Layer style shadows added

applying a filter to a stroke

This time, we'll leave the edges of the image alone and add a border over the top of it.

key concepts:

edit>stroke

filters

blending options

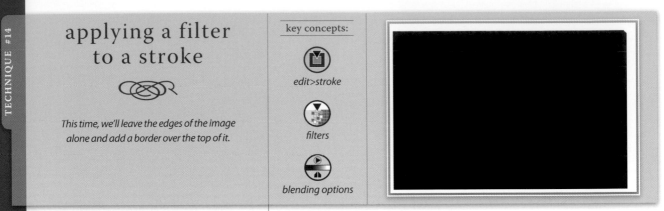

Step One:

Press Command-J (PC: Control-J) to duplicate the Background layer of your image. Then, use the Image>Canvas Size command, or press Command-Option-C (PC: Control-Alt-C), to add 2 inches of canvas (with the Relative checkbox turned on) to both the width and height.

Step Two:

Press-and-hold the Command key (PC: Control key) and click on the layer thumbnail of the copied layer (Layer 1) to make a selection of your image. Click on the Create a New Layer icon to add a blank layer above your copied image layer, and then choose Edit>Stroke. Use a fairly thick stroke width, and change the Location to Center. If appropriate, you can use a color you sample from a dark area of the photo, by clicking on the color swatch, and when the Color Picker comes up, moving your cursor over the photo and clicking on a dark color. Press Command-D (PC: Control-D) to Deselect.

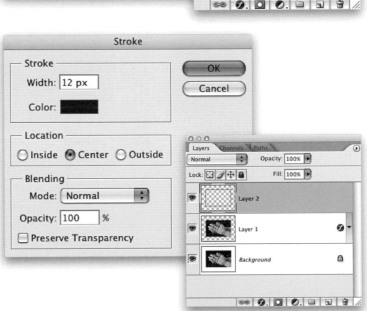

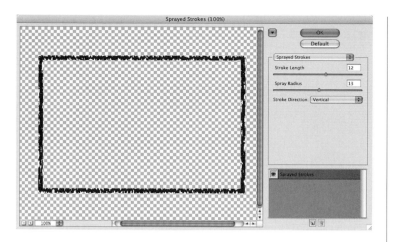

Step Three:

Now we'll apply a filter to the stroke. Here I used the Sprayed Strokes filter (under Filter>Brush Strokes). With many filters (like this one) some white areas are introduced, so we'll have to hide these areas in the next step.

Step Four:

Double-click on the stroke layer to open the Layer Style dialog. Blending Options: Default should be highlighted under Styles on the left side. Make sure your Blend If is set to Gray, then click on the white This Layer slider and drag it to the left so the white disappears. If the edges look too jagged, press-and-hold the Option key (PC: Alt key), click again on the slider, and drag left to split it. Now you can click-and-drag either side of the slider to soften the effect.

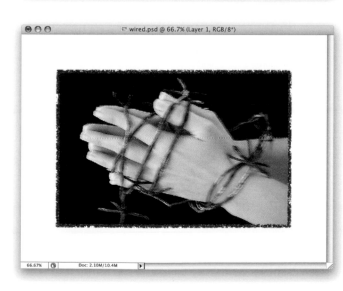

variations:

Here I added a second thin stroke in black around the image on a separate layer. You can do this by adding a new layer, and then using the Rectangular Marquee tool (M) to draw a selection slightly larger than your first stroke. Choose Edit>Stroke, reduce the Size, change the Color to black, and change the Location to Inside to get nice, square corners.

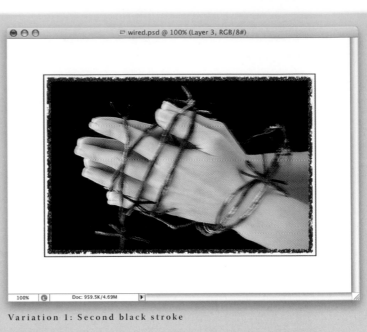

Variation 1: Second black stroke

Here's the same technique on a black background with a white stroke. To create the black background, simply add a new layer just above your Background layer, press D to set your Foreground and Background to their default colors, and press Option-Delete (PC: Alt-Backspace) to fill the layer with black.

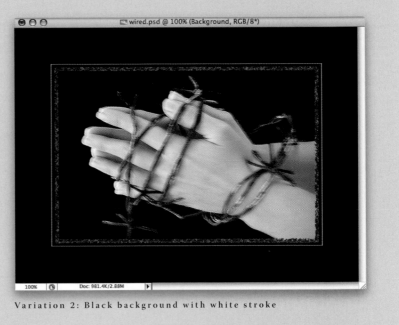

Variation 2: Black background with white stroke

Variation 3: Spatter filter applied to stroke with drop shadow

In this example, I applied a second filter (Brush Strokes>Spatter) to the thick brown stroke. Then, I used Free Transform (Command-T [PC: Control-T]) to distort the border—press-and-hold the Command key (PC: Control key) as you click-and-drag on the corner handles to distort—and added a Drop Shadow layer style.

applying filters
to shapes

In this technique, you'll use the
Rectangular Marquee and Polygonal
Lasso tools to create selections that
you'll fill with black, and then apply filters.

key concepts:

filters

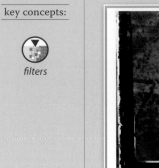

Step One:

Press Command-J (PC: Control-J) to duplicate the Background layer. Then use the
Image>Canvas Size command, or press Command-Option-C (PC: Control-Alt-C), to add 2
inches of canvas (with the Relative checkbox
turned on) to both the width and height. Click
on the Create a New Layer icon at the bottom
of the Layers palette to add a blank layer above
the photo layer. As an optional step, make sure
the copied photo layer is active, press-and-hold
the Command key (PC: Control key), and click
on the Create a New Layer icon to add a layer
below the copied photo layer that you can
fill with whatever color you want to use as
the background. Here I pressed D to set the
Foreground and Background to the default
colors and then pressed Command-Delete
(PC: Control-Backspace) to fill the new layer
with white.

Step Two:

Using the Rectangular Marquee tool (M), draw a selection across the top edge of your photo. If you haven't already, press D to set your Foreground color to black. Press Option-Delete (PC: Alt-Backspace) to fill your selection with black.

Step Three:

Continue creating shapes on all four sides of your photo and fill them with black. Use the Polygonal Lasso tool (press Shift-L until you get it) to create a more random shape. Use the Rectangular Marquee tool while pressing-and-holding the Shift key to add to the selection, or pressing-and-holding the Option key (PC: Alt key) to remove part of the selection.

Step Four:

Now you'll apply one or more filters to the border layer. In this example, from the Filter menu, I used Texture>Patchwork and Artistic>Paint Daubs.

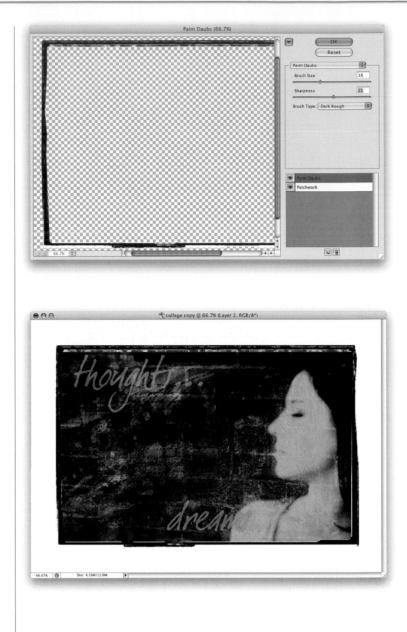

variations:

In this variation, I pressed Command-J (PC: Control-J) to duplicate the border layer. I then chose Filter>Blur and applied a slight Gaussian Blur to the original border layer. Then I changed the blend mode of the duplicated border layer to Linear Dodge.

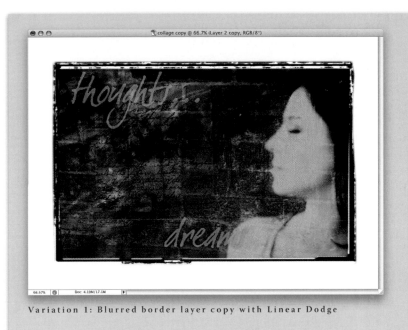

Variation 1: Blurred border layer copy with Linear Dodge

Here, I clicked on the Add a Layer Style icon at the bottom of the Layers palette and added a Color Overlay layer style to the original border layer (with a color sampled from the image and the Blend Mode changed to Color Dodge). Then I changed the blend mode of the duplicated border layer to Vivid Light.

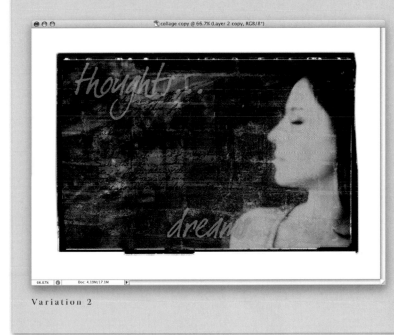

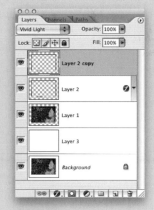

Variation 2

painting a border

This is a very simple technique with an amazing number of possibilities based on the brush you choose and blend mode you use. In this example, we'll use a photo on an angle, but of course this method will work for any photo. (In case you want to try it on a rotated photo, I'll cover those steps first. If you don't want your photo to be rotated then, well, don't rotate it!)

key concepts:

free transform

define brush

Step One:

Press Command-J (PC: Control-J) to duplicate the Background layer. Then use the Image>Canvas Size command, or press Command-Option-C (PC: Control-Alt-C), to add 1 inch of canvas (with the Relative checkbox turned on) to both the width and height.

Step Two:

Click on the top layer to make it active and then press Command-T (PC: Control-T) for Free Transform. Move your cursor just outside the corner transform handles until you see the Rotate cursor, click-and-drag to rotate the photo slightly, and then press Return (PC: Enter). In my example, I pressed D to set the Foreground and Background to their default colors, clicked on the Background layer, and pressed Option-Delete (PC: Alt-Backspace) to fill it with black. Or, with the Background layer active, you could click on the Create a New Layer icon (at the bottom of the Layers palette) to add a new layer above the Background layer, and then fill that new layer with black.

Step Three:

Get the Brush tool (B), and click on the Brush thumbnail in the Options Bar to bring up the Brush Picker. Here's where you need to be prepared to experiment a bit, tweaking the Brush tool settings to get the effect you want. In this example, from the Brush Picker I chose a brush tip called Oil Medium to Large Tip after choosing the Wet Media Brushes set from the flyout menu. Then I made a bunch of modifications (pimp my brush?) in the Brushes palette (which is docked in the Palette Well by default). I changed a number of settings, including Shape Dynamics, and for a texture pattern I used a pattern that I had created earlier from another photo. (This, in part, explains why your brush will not look the same as mine.)

> **TIP**
>
> Once you have gone to the trouble of creating a custom brush, you can save that brush for future use by going to Edit>Preset Manager. In the Preset Manager dialog, choose Brushes from the Preset Type pop-up menu, press-and-hold the Command key (PC: Control key), and click on your custom brushes. Then click Save Set and save them somewhere on your computer so you can load the brushes back in at any time.

Step Four:

Click on the Create a New Layer icon to add a new layer above the photo layer. Choose the Brush tool and then choose your custom brush from the Brush Picker. After choosing a contrasting Foreground color (I used gray), click once on a corner of your photo, press-and-hold the Shift key, and click on the opposite corner. Repeat this operation until you have painted a border around the edges of your photo.

Needless to say, with different brush tips and different settings you can get all kinds of different effects. And don't forget, you can also try creating your own brushes and using those. (See the Key Concepts section for details on creating brushes.)

variations:

Changing blend modes will have a major impact on the end result. Here are some examples where I simply changed the blend mode of the painted border layer.

Variation 1: Linear Dodge blend mode

Variation 2: Screen blend mode

Variation 3: Difference blend mode

Variation 4: Hard Light blend mode

In Variation 6, I added another layer, chose a different brush, a darker gray, and painted a second border that I then rotated slightly with Free Transform. Then I changed the blend mode of the top border layer to Color Burn.

Variation 5: Linear Light blend mode

Variation 6: Second, darker border added

key concepts:

define brush

painting along a path

Here we'll use a technique similar to one we used earlier to alter a layer mask. We'll create a path and then paint along that path to create a border.

Step One:

Press Command-J (PC: Control-J) to duplicate the Background layer. Then use the Image>Canvas Size command, or press Command-Option-C (PC: Control-Alt-C), to add 1 inch of canvas (with the Relative checkbox turned on) to both the width and height. Click on the Create a New Layer icon at the bottom of the layers palette to add a new layer on top of the copied Background layer. This is where you'll add the border.

115

Step Two:

Press-and-hold the Command key (PC: Control key) and click on the thumbnail of the copied Background layer (Layer 1, in my example) to create a selection of your image. Then switch to the Paths palette (nested behind the Layers palette by default) and from the flyout menu, choose Make Work Path. In the resulting dialog, enter a Tolerance of 0.5 pixels.

Step Three:

Choose the Brush tool (B) and, in the Options Bar, pick a brush shape from the Brush Picker, then set the brush opacity. In this example, I used a 66-pixel brush called Dry Brush Tip Light Flow from the default set of brushes, but don't forget you can always tweak your brush in the Brushes palette. Click on the Foreground color swatch at the bottom of the Toolbox, and from the resulting Color Picker, choose the color you want to use. I used black in this case.

Step Four:

Make sure the blank layer is active and then switch back to the Paths palette. Press-and-hold the Option key (PC: Alt key) and click on the Stroke Path with Brush icon (second from the left at the bottom of the Paths palette). In the Stroke Path dialog, choose Brush from the Tool pop-up menu, if it is not already selected, and turn on the Simulate Pressure checkbox. Click OK and the brush will paint along the path (on the active layer).

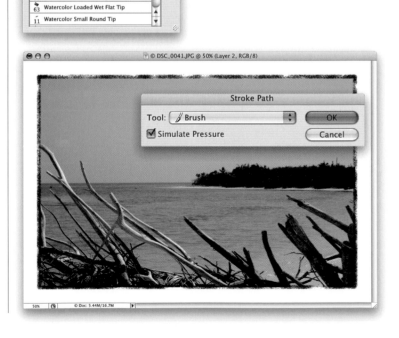

variations:

In this example, I repeated Steps Three and Four, but this time used the Airbrush Dual Brush Soft Round 45 brush.

Variation 1: Airbrush Dual Brush Soft Round 45 brush

Here I changed the blend mode of the border layer to Color Burn, so that the border only appears over the photo.

Variation 2: Color Burn blend mode

painting and smudging along a path

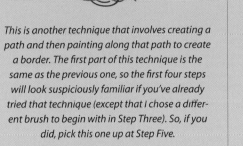

key concepts:

define brush

This is another technique that involves creating a path and then painting along that path to create a border. The first part of this technique is the same as the previous one, so the first four steps will look suspiciously familiar if you've already tried that technique (except that I chose a different brush to begin with in Step Three). So, if you did, pick this one up at Step Five.

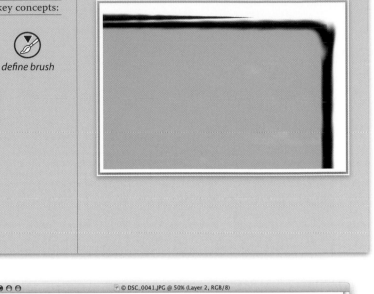

Step One:

Press Command-J (PC: Control-J) to duplicate the Background layer. Then use the Image>Canvas Size command, or press Command-Option-C (PC: Control-Alt-C), to add 1 inch of canvas (with the Relative checkbox turned on) to both the width and height. Click on the Create a New Layer icon at the bottom of the layers palette to add a new layer on top of the copied Background layer. This is where you'll add the border.

Step Two:

Press-and-hold the Command key (PC: Control key) and click on the thumbnail of the copied Background layer (Layer 1, in my example) to create a selection. Then switch to the Paths palette (found nested behind the Layers palette by default) and from the flyout menu, choose Make Work Path. In the resulting dialog, enter a Tolerance of 0.5 pixels.

Step Three:

Choose the Brush tool (B) and, in the Options Bar, pick a brush shape from the Brush Picker, then set the brush opacity. In this example, I used a brush called Airbrush Dual Brush Soft Round 45 from the default set of brushes. (Remember, you can always tweak the brush settings in the Brushes palette.) Click on the Foreground color swatch at the bottom of the Toolbox, and from the resulting Color Picker, choose the color you want to use. I used black in this case.

Step Four:

Make sure the blank layer is active and then switch back to the Paths palette. Press-and-hold the Option key (PC: Alt key) and click on the Stroke Path with Brush icon (second from the left at the bottom of the Paths palette). In the Stroke Path dialog, choose Brush from the Tool pop-up menu, if it is not already selected, and turn on the Simulate Pressure checkbox. Click OK and the brush will paint along the path (on the active layer).

Step Five:

On the bottom right of the Paths palette, click on the Create New Path icon to create (guess what?) a new path. Choose the Pen tool (P), and in the Options Bar make sure that the Path icon (the second from the left) is active. With the Pen tool, make three points: click once on the left side of the image beside the existing border (1), then move up to the top-left corner and click again (2), then move over towards the top-right corner and click again (3), and then press Return (PC: Enter). Don't worry about trying to make straight lines and, of course, you can create any length of path that you want.

Step Six:

In the Layers palette, click on the Create a New Layer icon to create another new layer and, again, switch back to the Paths palette. With the new path active, press-and-hold the Option key (PC: Alt key) and click on the Stroke Path with Brush icon. In the Stroke Path dialog, choose Brush from the Tool pop-up menu, if it is not already selected, and turn on the Simulate Pressure checkbox. Click OK and the brush will paint along the path (on the active layer).

You can also build on this technique by smudging the border. To do this, first choose the Smudge tool (R) and then enter the settings you want in the Options Bar. (Here you can see the settings I used in this example.) Activate one of the border layers, switch to the Paths palette, and make sure the path is also active. Press-and-hold the Option key (PC: Alt key) and click on the Stroke Path with Brush icon. In the Stroke Path dialog, choose Smudge from the Tool pop-up menu, if it is not already selected, turn on the Simulate Pressure checkbox, and click OK. Here's the result after applying the smudge along the path twice.

variations:

In this variation, I added a Gradient Overlay layer style to both border layers by clicking on the Add a Layer Style icon (at the bottom of the Layers palette) and including the settings shown here.

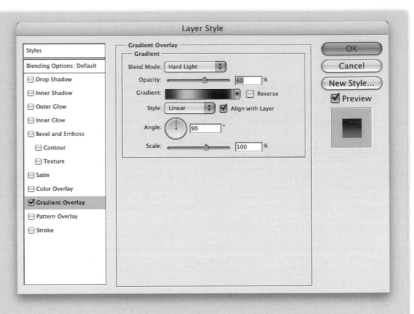

Variation 1: Gradient Overlay layer style

Variation 2

Here I held down the Command key (PC: Control key) and clicked on both border layers to activate them. Then I chose Merge Visible from the Layers palette's flyout menu to merge the two border layers. I then duplicated the result, filled the duplicated layer with a shade of orange, and changed the layer blend mode to Overlay. (*Hint:* To fill only the border with the Foreground color, press Option-Shift-Delete [PC: Alt-Shift-Backspace].)

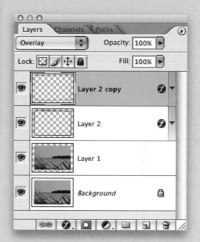

using borders from illustrator

If you're a lucky owner of Illustrator CS2, you can create some great borders that can easily be used in Photoshop in a very scalable way. (If you don't have Illustrator, move on. There's nothing to see here.)

key concepts:

illustrator to photoshop

free transform

layer styles

Step One:

As we've done in many of the techniques, you'll start by pressing Command-J (PC: Control-J) to duplicate the Background layer. Then use the Image>Canvas Size command, or press Command-Option-C (PC: Control-Alt-C), to add 1 inch of canvas (with the Relative checkbox turned on) to both the width and height. Finally, press-and-hold the Command key (PC: Control key) and click on the Create a New Layer icon at the bottom of the layers palette to add a new layer below the copied Background layer. In this case, I clicked on the Foreground color swatch at the bottom of the Toolbox, chose a shade of gray, and pressed Option-Delete (PC: Alt-Backspace) to fill this new layer with gray. I did this because my photo had a very light background and I wanted to see the edges of the image. (Depending on the image, you can also fill the new layer with white, if you choose.)

Step Two:

In Illustrator, use the Pen tool (P) to create a horizontal path that's approximately the width of your image. If you're not sure, guess, because you'll be able to scale the object in Photoshop. Select the path and copy it to the Clipboard (Command-C [PC: Control-C]).

Step Three:

Switch back to your Photoshop document and make sure that the copied Background layer is active. Press D to set your Foreground color to black. Choose Edit>Paste and select Shape Layer in the resulting Paste dialog. (If you forget to set your Foreground color to black before you paste, just double-click on the Shape layer thumbnail to open the Color Picker.) If the Shape layer is not the right size, press Command-T (PC: Control-T) and use Free Transform to change it to the appropriate size.

Step Four:

Repeat this operation for all sides of your image, experimenting with different brushes in Illustrator to create horizontal and vertical borders.

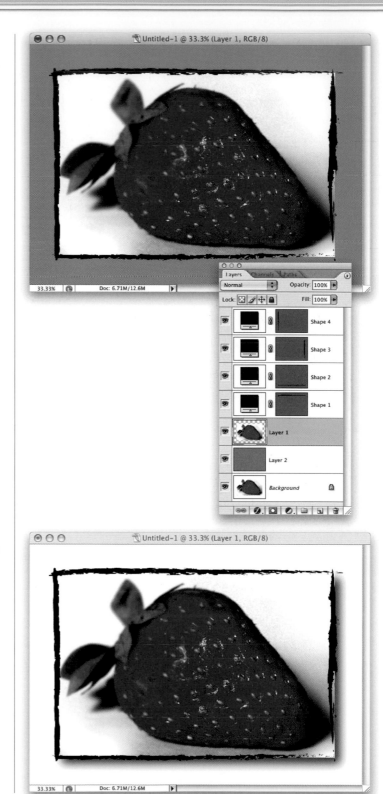

Here's the finished product. I pressed Command-Delete (PC: Control-Backspace) to change the underlying layer (Layer 2) to white. Then I clicked on the Add a Layer Style icon (at the bottom of the Layers palette) and added a soft, offset drop shadow to the photo layer (Layer 1).

Variation 1: Pasting as a Smart Object

variation:

If you want a bit more flexibility in editing the Illustrator shapes, choose Smart Object when you Paste in Photoshop. This creates a live link from Photoshop back to the original Illustrator artwork. Just double-click on the Smart Object icon in the Layers palette to edit the artwork in Illustrator. When you save and close the Illustrator document and return to Photoshop, the artwork will update (while preserving the position and scale of the pasted border).

defining a border brush

This time you'll define large brushes from a textured photo and use those brushes to click once and paint a border. (Use a textured photo that's at least as large, or larger than, the photo to which you'll add the border.)

key concepts:

define brush

layer styles

layer masks

Step One:

Open your textured photo and with the Rectangular Marquee tool (M) make a selection that's at least as wide (or wider) than your destination photo. *Note:* A brush cannot be defined from a selection larger than 2500 pixels, so make sure your selection is less than that size.

Step Two:

From the Edit menu, choose Define Brush Preset. In the resulting dialog, name the brush, and click OK. Make another selection, but this time make a vertical selection that you'll use for the sides of the image. Again, choose Edit>Define Brush Preset and name the brush.

Step Three:

Open the image to which you want to add the border and press Command-J (PC: Control-J) to duplicate the Background layer. Then use the Image>Canvas Size command, or press Command-Option-C (PC: Control-Alt-C), to add 1 inch of canvas (with the Relative checkbox turned on) to both the width and height. To add a bit more depth to the image, I also added a drop shadow by clicking on the Add a Layer Style icon at the bottom of the Layers palette and choosing Drop Shadow.

Step Four:

Click on the Create a New Layer icon at the bottom of the Layers palette to add a new layer on top of the copied Background layer. This is where you'll add the border. Press B to activate the Brush tool, click on the Brush thumbnail in the Options Bar, and from the Brush Picker, choose your wide (horizontal) brush that you defined in Step Two. Click on the Foreground color swatch in the Toolbox to choose your color from the Color Picker (I used black in this example). Then, position the cursor along the top edge of the photo. If the brush is too big, press the Left Bracket key ([) repeatedly to make the brush the size you need. Click once to paint a border with your custom brush. Depending on the texture in your brush, you may want to move the brush slightly up or down and left or right, and click a second time. Repeat the process along the bottom edge of the photo.

Step Five:

Continue painting with this one-click method, this time using the vertical brush you defined in Step Two. In my example, I lowered the opacity slightly (in the Options Bar) and clicked three times to overlay several painted borders. I also used the Brushes palette (docked in the Palette Well by default) to rotate the vertical brush very slightly and, again, painted several overlapping borders. You'll notice that I deliberately painted borders that were bigger than I needed.

Step Six:

If you want the border to only appear within the photo, Command-click (PC: Control-click) on the copied Background layer's thumbnail (Layer 1, in my example), and then click on the Add Layer Mask icon at the bottom of the Layers palette.

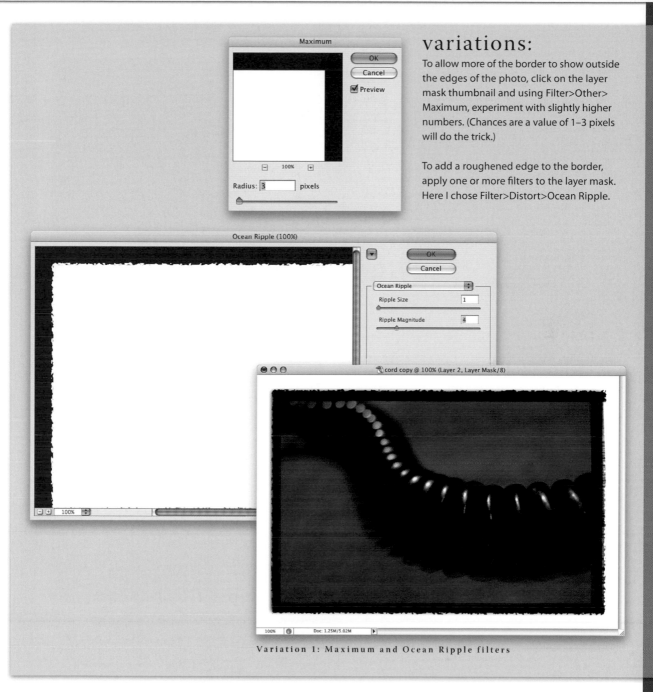

variations:

To allow more of the border to show outside the edges of the photo, click on the layer mask thumbnail and using Filter>Other> Maximum, experiment with slightly higher numbers. (Chances are a value of 1–3 pixels will do the trick.)

To add a roughened edge to the border, apply one or more filters to the layer mask. Here I chose Filter>Distort>Ocean Ripple.

Variation 1: Maximum and Ocean Ripple filters

131

You can also create a roughened edge on the inside of your border, too. Command-click (PC: Control-click) on the border layer's thumbnail.

Variation 2

Press Q to enter Quick Mask mode and apply a filter (Ocean Ripple again, in this case). Press Q again, to go back to Standard mode.

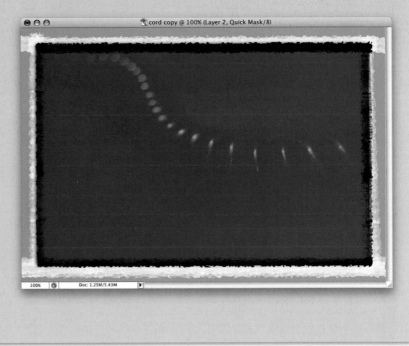

Click on the Create a New Layer icon to add a layer at the top of the layer stack, and press Option-Delete (PC: Alt-Backspace) to fill it with black. Press-and-hold the Option key (PC: Alt key) and click-and-drag to copy the existing layer mask onto this new layer.

TECHNIQUE #20

defining a threshold border

This time, you'll use a textured photo and the Threshold command to select areas to use as borders. (Use a textured photo that's at least as large, or larger than, the photo to which you'll add the border.)

key concepts:

threshold

free transform

quick mask

blend modes

filters

layer masks

layer styles

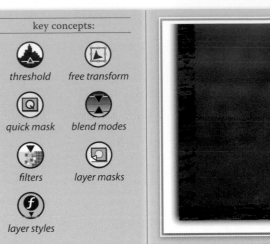

Step One:

Open your textured photo and from the Image menu, choose Adjustments>Threshold. Move the slider until you get an interesting black-and-white texture (refer to Key Concepts for more details).

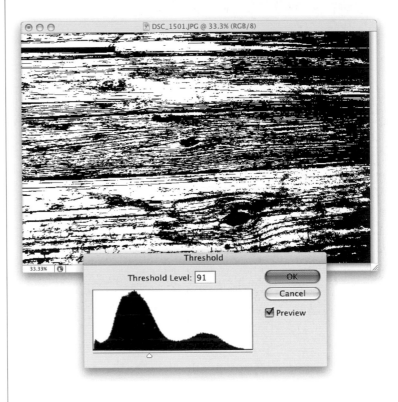

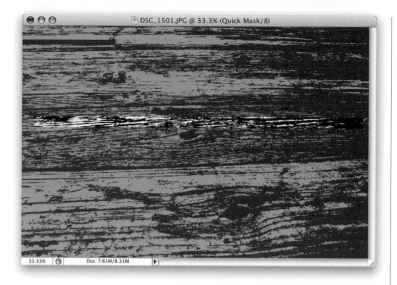

Step Two:

With the Rectangular Marquee tool (M), make a selection that's at least as wide as (or wider than) your destination photo. Press Q to enter Quick Mask mode to help isolate your selection and see what kind of border you'll get.

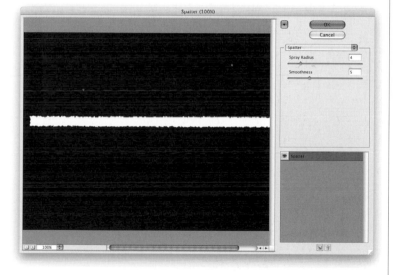

Step Three:

As an optional step, while in Quick Mask mode, you can apply a distortion filter such as Brush Strokes>Spatter to create a more randomized edge. After applying the filter, press Q again to return to Standard mode and then press Command-C (PC: Control-C) to Copy the selection.

Step Four:

Switch to your photo and press Command-J (PC: Control-J) to duplicate the Background layer. Then use the Image>Canvas Size command, or press Command-Option-C (PC: Control-Alt-C), to add 1 inch of canvas (with the Relative checkbox turned on) to both the width and height. To add a bit more depth to the image, I also added a drop shadow by clicking on the Add a Layer Style icon at the bottom of the Layers palette and choosing Drop Shadow.

Step Five:

Press Command-V (PC: Control-V) to Paste the selected area from the textured photo. Press Command-T (PC: Control-T) to go into Free Transform mode, and scale the texture layer down to make it slightly larger than your photo. Return to the textured photo and repeat Steps Two, Three, and Five to make additional selections and paste them into the photo (of course, you'll end up making two horizontal and two vertical selections).

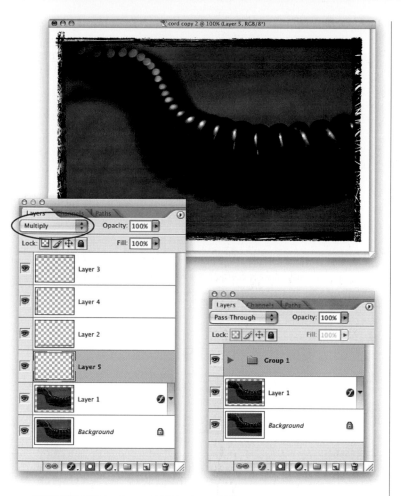

Step Six:

Change the blend mode of each of the border layers to Multiply to remove the white pixels in the borders. *Hint:* Command-click (PC: Control-click) on each of the border layers to select them and then from the Layers palette's flyout menu, choose New Group from Layers. That will create a Group (folder) that contains the four border layers.

Step Seven:

If you want the borders to only appear on the photo (with a sharp edge at the edges of the photo), Command-click (PC: Control-click) on the photo layer thumbnail. Then click on the Group layer to activate it and click on the Add Layer Mask icon at the bottom of the Layers palette to add a layer mask to the Group.

variations:

Choose Filter>Other>Maximum to make the white area of the layer mask slightly larger, allowing more of the borders to show.

Variation 1: Maximum filter

Apply a filter to the layer mask to create a more random edge to the border layers (here I used Distort>Glass).

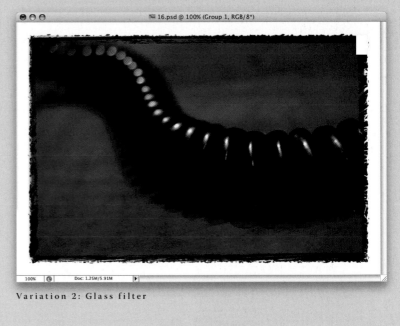

Variation 2: Glass filter

key concepts:

threshold

free transform

blending options

drawing your own border

If you don't have access to a scanner, you can also draw an edge (or portions of one), take a photograph of it, and turn that into a border.

Step One:

Press Command-J (PC: Control-J) to duplicate the Background layer, and then press Command-Option-C (PC: Control-Alt-C) to open the Canvas Size dialog. Make sure the Relative checkbox is turned on, and add 1 inch to both the width and the height.

Step Two:

Open the scanned image or photo you took of the edge that you drew—as you can see in this example, having great lighting is not important.

139

Step Three:

Under the Image menu, choose Adjustments>
Threshold and drag the slider to the left until
you get the result you want. Here you can see
two examples of the edge I drew.

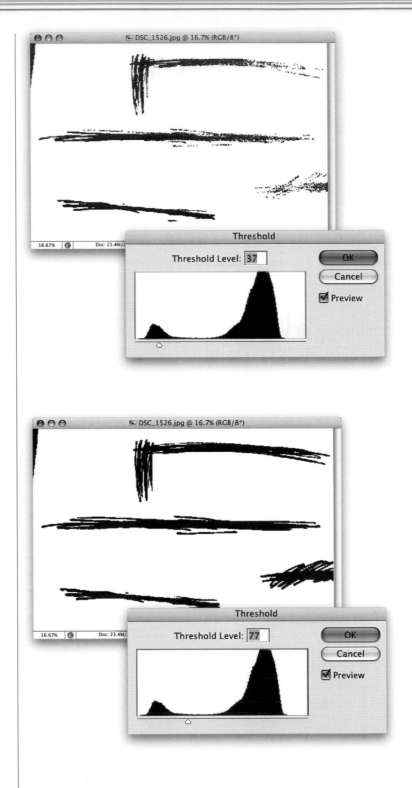

Step Four:

Using the Rectangular Marquee tool (M), select one of the areas you'll use as a border. Copy-and-paste it onto your photograph. In this example, I scaled and rotated the copied pixels using Free Transform (Command-T [PC: Control-T]) to add a vertical border on one side. Initially, the copied border will have a white background.

Step Five:

Double-click on the border layer to edit the Blending Options in the Layer Style dialog. In the Blend If section, drag the white slider under This Layer to the left and the white background of the layer will become transparent. If you then press-and-hold the Option key (PC: Alt key) while you click-and-drag the slider, it will split, allowing you to create a smoother edge on the black pixels.

Step Six:

Repeat Steps Four and Five until you have borders on all sides. Chances are you'll end up with more than four border layers, as each side may require more than one piece.

If you wish, you can put the borders into a Group (folder) so that you can show or hide them in one step. To do this, select all the border layers (by Shift-clicking on the first one, then Shift-clicking on the last one), and then in the Layers palette's flyout menu, choose New Group from Layers.

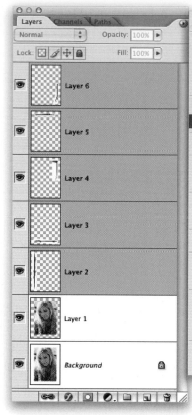

In order to add layer styles to our borders we have to merge them together (otherwise the white backgrounds would come into play). In this example, I duplicated the Group so that I could keep the separate border layers in the original and have a copy in which I could merge the layers. After copying the Group (by choosing Duplicate Group from the Layers palette's flyout menu), I selected the border layers in the Group and chose Merge Layers from the flyout menu.

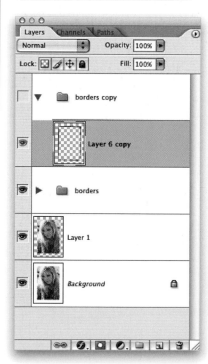

Variation 1

variation:

In this variation, I added a layer style to the merged border layer by clicking on the Add a Layer Style icon at the bottom of the Layers palette and choosing Gradient Overlay, then changing the Blend Mode to Vivid Light.

gallery print

Scott Kelby coined the name "gallery print" for this effect, since it adds a "we bought this from a high-end gallery" look. It's easy to do, and you could even record an action with these steps to automate the whole thing. (If you wanted to make this into an action, you would simply start recording before you did these steps.)

key concepts:

free transform

edit>stroke

layer styles

DAVE CROSS

Step One:

Press Command-J (PC: Control-J) to duplicate the Background layer.

Step Two:

From the Image menu, choose Canvas Size (or press Command-Option-C [PC: Control-Alt-C]). Make sure the Relative checkbox is turned on and add 1 inch to both the width and height (or more if you prefer).

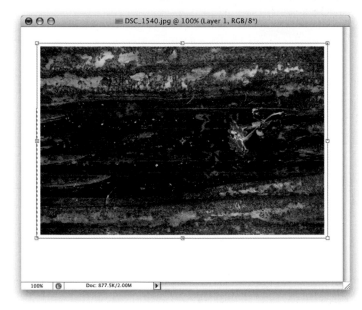

Step Three:

Then, choose Image>Canvas Size again, and this time click in the top-center square of the Anchor grid to add canvas only to the bottom. We'll add .75 to just the height (this is assuming that you want to add some text as we will in Step Seven—if you don't want any text, skip this step and Step Seven).

Step Four:

Command-click (PC: Control-click) on the thumbnail of the top layer to load the image as a selection. Then from the Select menu, choose Transform Selection. Press-and-hold the Option key (PC: Alt key) and click-and-drag one of the corner handles slightly outwards to make the selection slightly larger than the image. (Holding down the Option key resizes the selection from the center.) Press Return (PC: Enter) when you're done.

Although you could use Select>Modify>Expand to make the selection larger, I don't recommend it, as the corners of the selection will become slightly rounded. You can make the selection larger by using Transform Selection and entering slightly larger values in the fields in the Options Bar. Control-click (PC: Right-click) on the Width field and choose pixels from the contextual menu. Repeat for the Height field and then enter values in each of these fields, adding whatever amount you want (e.g., add 10 pixels to each value).

Step Five:

Click on the Create a New Layer icon at the bottom of the Layers palette to add a new layer. From the Edit menu, choose Stroke, and use a width of 1 or 2 pixels with Inside as the Location. I used black for the Color here but you could use a dark gray, too. Click OK, and then press Command-D (PC: Control-D) to Deselect.

Step Six:

As an optional step, I'll add a slight drop shadow to the stroke layer. With the stroke layer active, click on the Add a Layer Style icon at the bottom of the Layers palette and choose Drop Shadow from the pop-up menu. Enter a small value for the distance and size.

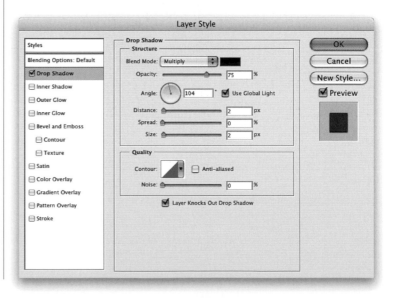

Step Seven:

Finally, use the Type tool (T) to add center-aligned text under the image (click the Center Text icon in the Options Bar to align it). After entering the text, I increased the tracking dramatically (by pressing Option-Right Arrow [PC: Alt-Right Arrow]) to loosen the spacing between the letters.

Hint: To align the Type layer with the photo, Command-click (PC: Control-click) on both layers to select them, choose the Move tool (V), and click on the Align Horizontal Centers icon in the Options Bar.

variations:

Here's a slight variation on the same theme, on a black background with the stroke and text changed to white.

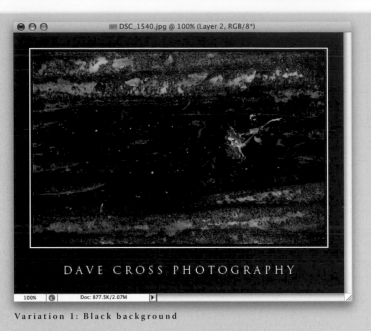

Variation 1: Black background

Try lowering the opacity of the stroke and/or the type.

Variation 2: Lowered opacity of stroke and type

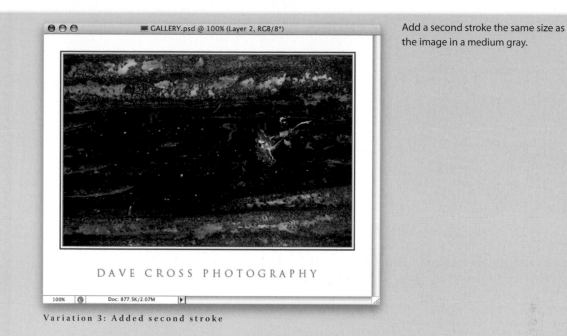

Add a second stroke the same size as the image in a medium gray.

Variation 3: Added second stroke

layer style border

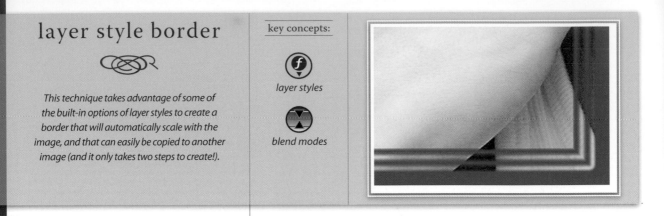

This technique takes advantage of some of the built-in options of layer styles to create a border that will automatically scale with the image, and that can easily be copied to another image (and it only takes two steps to create!).

key concepts:

layer styles

blend modes

Step One:

Since you cannot apply a layer style to the Background layer, you'll have to rename the layer. The simplest way is to press-and-hold the Option key (PC: Alt key) and double-click on the Background layer—this will name the layer "Layer 0." (If you want to name the layer something else, don't hold down the Option key and you'll get a dialog asking you to enter a name for the layer.)

Step Two:

Click on the Add a Layer Style icon at the bottom of the Layers palette, and from the pop-up menu choose Inner Glow. You can experiment with a number of settings here, but the key ones are Blend Mode, Color, Choke, and Size. In this example, I used a golden brown as the color, changed the Blend Mode to Normal, added 14% Noise, set the Choke to 29%, and the Size to 65 pixels. (The blend mode defaults to Screen, which is fine for traditional inner glows, but you'll need to change it to Normal to create a more noticeable border.)

variations:

Try different Contour settings to create multi-line borders. Here I used the contour called Ring and reduced the Noise to 0%.

Variation 1: Ring contour

In this case, the additional contours were loaded from the Contour Picker's flyout menu. I used Ring—Triple.

Variation 2: Ring—Triple contour

In this example, after adding the layer style I increased the canvas size and added a white layer below the photo layer. To do this, press Command-Option-C (PC: Control-Alt-C) to bring up the Canvas Size dialog, and add as much canvas as you like. Then, Command-click (PC: Control-click) on the Create a New Layer icon. Press D to set your Foreground and Background colors to their defaults, and press Command-Delete (PC: Control-Backspace) to fill the layer with white.

Variation 3

As mentioned, one of the advantages of using a layer style to create a border is how well it transfers to another image, even when the photo is a different size, resolution, or orientation (as in this example). To transfer it to another image, simply click on the layer style icon (the small *f*) in the Layers palette and drag it onto your other image (you will have to rename the Background layer in that image or copy the image to a new layer, since you can't add a layer style to the Background layer).

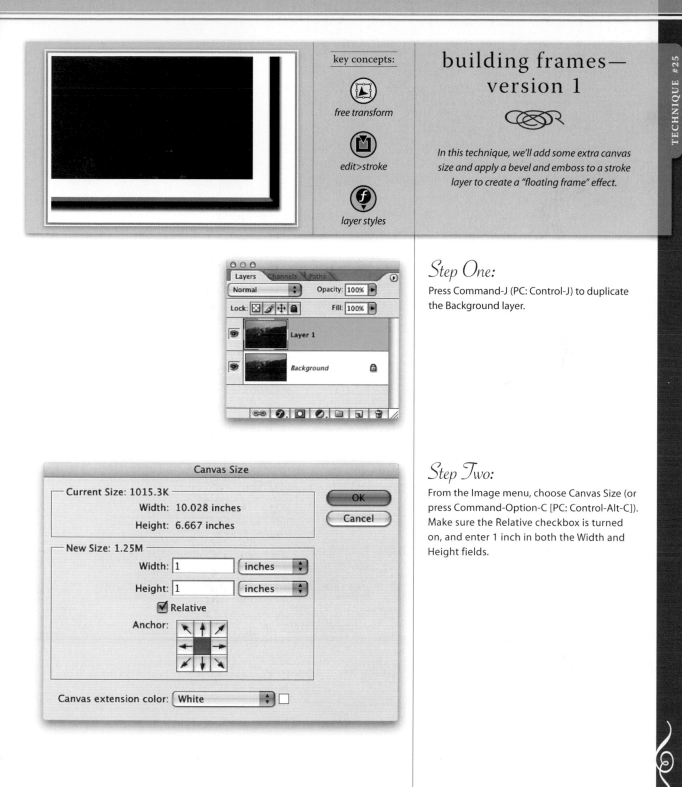

key concepts:

free transform

edit>stroke

layer styles

building frames—
version 1

In this technique, we'll add some extra canvas size and apply a bevel and emboss to a stroke layer to create a "floating frame" effect.

Step One:

Press Command-J (PC: Control-J) to duplicate the Background layer.

Step Two:

From the Image menu, choose Canvas Size (or press Command-Option-C [PC: Control-Alt-C]). Make sure the Relative checkbox is turned on, and enter 1 inch in both the Width and Height fields.

Layers panel:

Normal — Opacity: 100%
Lock: — Fill: 100%
Layer 1
Background

Canvas Size

Current Size: 1015.3K
Width: 10.028 inches
Height: 6.667 inches

New Size: 1.25M
Width: 1 inches
Height: 1 inches
☑ Relative
Anchor:

Canvas extension color: White

OK
Cancel

Step Three:

Press-and-hold the Command key (PC: Control key) and click on the Create a New Layer icon at the bottom of the Layers palette to create a layer below the current layer. Fill the new layer with white by pressing D to set your Foreground and Background colors to the default, then pressing Command-Delete (PC: Control-Backspace).

Step Four:

Press-and-hold the Command key (PC: Control key) and click on the thumbnail for the duplicated photo layer (Layer 1, in this example) to load it as a selection. From the Select menu, choose Transform Selection and while pressing-and-holding the Option key (PC: Alt key), click on a corner handle and drag the box outwards. Make the selection considerably larger than the photo.

> **NOTE**
>
> It is tempting to use the settings in the Options Bar to scale the selection by percentage, but be careful: if you use the same percentage for both width and height, the selection will not be even (unless you have a square photo). I would certainly never claim to be a mathematician, but with some experimentation I found that using 107% for the width and 110.5% for the height produced the result I was looking for. (*Disclaimer:* This is only a guideline—your results may vary. Follow manufacturer's instructions for best results.)

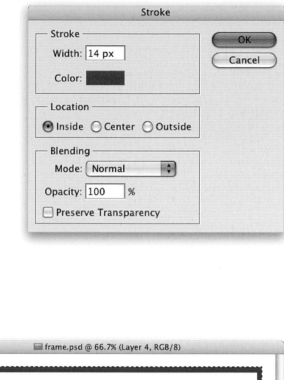

Step Five:

Click on the Create a New Layer icon to add a new layer at the top of the layer stack, and from the Edit menu choose Stroke. Enter a large width (I used 14 pixels), set the Location to Inside, and choose a medium-to-dark gray color (click on the color swatch to bring up the Color Picker). Click OK and press Command-D (PC: Control-D) to Deselect.

Step Six:

With the stroke layer still active, click on the Add a Layer Style icon at the bottom of the Layers palette and choose Bevel and Emboss from the pop-up menu. Change the Technique to Chisel Hard and increase the Size setting slightly.

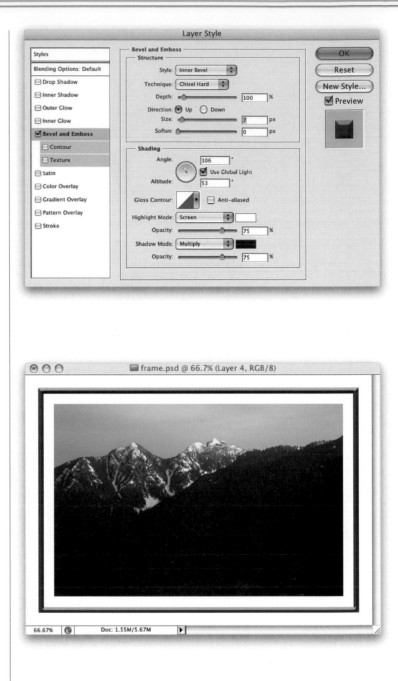

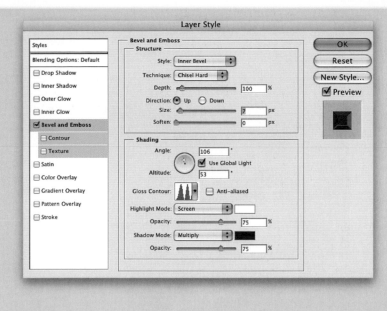

variations:

In this example, I changed the Gloss Contour setting in the Bevel and Emboss layer style to Peaks.

Variation 1: Peaks contour

Here, I changed the white layer below the photo layer to black. To do this, simply press D to set the Foreground to black and press Option-Delete (PC: Alt-Backspace) to fill the layer with your Foreground color.

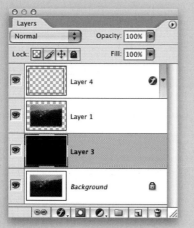

Variation 2: Black background

This version has a gray layer below the photo (click on the Foreground color swatch at the bottom of the Toolbox and choose a medium gray from the Color Picker), and the stroke layer was changed to a much darker gray.

Variation 3: Gray background with darker gray stroke

key concepts:

layer masks

layer styles

building frames—version 2

Here we'll use a built-in pattern and the Bevel and Emboss layer style to create a wood frame effect.

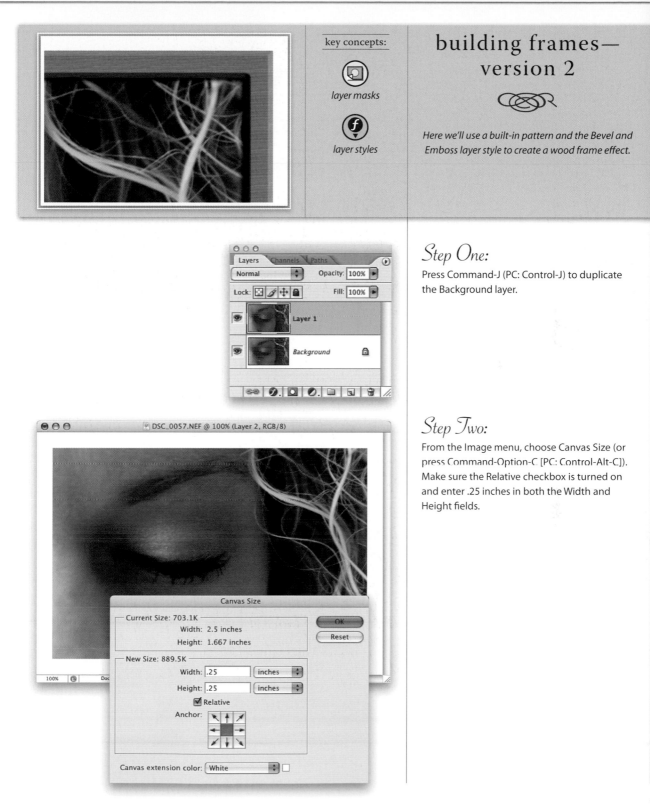

Step One:

Press Command-J (PC: Control-J) to duplicate the Background layer.

Step Two:

From the Image menu, choose Canvas Size (or press Command-Option-C [PC: Control-Alt-C]). Make sure the Relative checkbox is turned on and enter .25 inches in both the Width and Height fields.

Step Three:

Click on the Create a New Layer icon at the bottom of the Layers palette to add a new layer above the photo layer and, from the Edit menu, choose Fill. In the Fill dialog, choose Pattern from the Use pop-up menu and pick the built-in pattern called Wood from the Custom Pattern Picker. Make sure the Mode is Normal and the Opacity is 100%. (This will temporarily cover up our photo, but we'll fix that next.) With the wood layer still active, press-and-hold the Command key (PC: Control key) and click on the thumbnail of the photo layer to load a selection of that size.

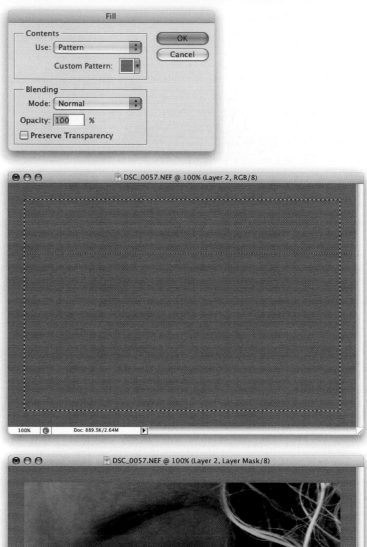

Step Four:

Next, press-and-hold the Option key (PC: Alt key) and click on the Add Layer Mask icon at the bottom of the Layers palette. This will create a layer mask that hides the center of the wood layer, leaving a frame around your photo.

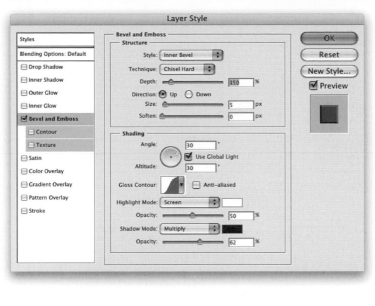

Step Five:

Click on the wood layer thumbnail to activate the layer (rather than the mask), then click on the Add a Layer Style icon at the bottom of the Layers palette and choose Bevel and Emboss from the pop-up menu to add dimension to the wood layer. Change the Technique to Chisel Hard, the Depth to 150%, and lower the Opacity settings for the Highlight and Shadow Modes. Click on the Gloss Contour thumbnail and choose Gaussian from the Contour Picker.

Step Six:

Click on the photo layer to activate it, and using the Add a Layer Style pop-up menu, add an Inner Shadow to the photo. Change the Blend Mode Opacity to 67%, and increase the Choke to 4%.

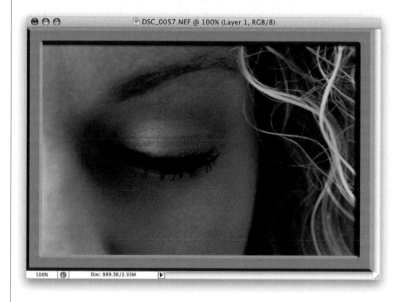

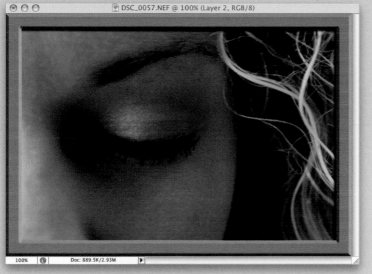

Variation 1: Steep Slope—Jagged contour

variations:

In this example, I changed the Gloss Contour setting in the Bevel and Emboss layer style to Steep Slope—Jagged.

Here I added a Color Overlay layer style to the wood layer, chose a dark brown as the color, and set its Blend Mode to Color Burn.

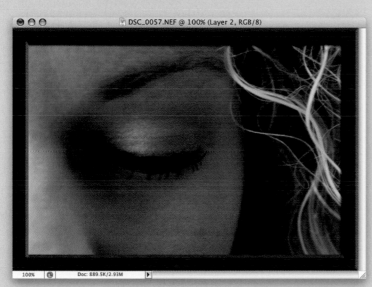

Variation 2: Color Overlay and Color Burn

two-photo effect

This technique offers a wide range of possibilities, but starts with a very simple premise: use the same photo twice.

key concepts:

free transform

adjustment layers

stroke layer style

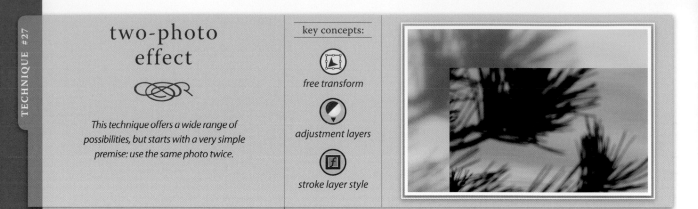

Step One:

Press Command-J (PC: Control-J) to duplicate the Background layer.

Step Two:

Press Command-T (PC: Control-T) to enter Free Transform mode. Then, Option-Shift-click (PC: Alt-Shift-click) on a corner handle and drag towards the center. This will scale down the photo and keep it centered. Press Return (PC: Enter) to commit the transformation.

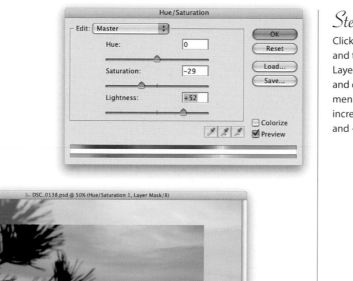

Step Three:

Click on the Background layer to make it active, and then click on the Create New Adjustment Layer icon at the bottom of the Layers palette, and choose Hue/Saturation from the pop-up menu. Lower the Saturation slightly and increase the Lightness (I used -29 for Saturation and +52 for Lightness). Click OK.

Step Four:

Click on the scaled photo layer to activate it, then click on the Add a Layer Style icon at the bottom of the Layers palette and choose Stroke from the pop-up menu. In the Layer Style dialog, click on the color swatch, then move your cursor onto the photo and use the eyedropper to choose a color from the image. (Make sure the Position is set to Inside.)

variations:

To create a soft focus effect on the larger background image, I duplicated the Background layer, and using the Filter menu, applied a Gaussian Blur of 10, and then lowered the opacity of the blurry layer to 70%.

Variation 1: Gaussian Blur applied to background

Here I made a selection based on the smaller photo by Command-clicking (PC: Control-clicking) on its thumbnail in the Layers palette, then adding a layer on which I created a stroke (using Edit>Stroke). Then, I applied a filter to the stroke layer. (See Technique #14 for the steps to apply a filter to a stroke.)

Variation 2: Filter applied to stroke

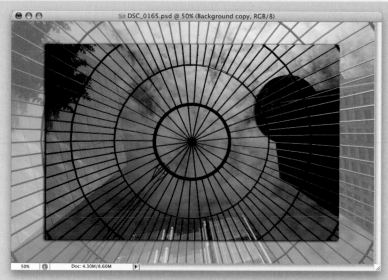

DSC_0165.psd @ 50% (Background copy, RGB/8)

50%   Doc: 4.30M/8.60M

Variation 3: Stroke replaced with drop shadow

In this example, I scaled the smaller photo, added the Hue/Saturation adjustment layer, and then added a Drop Shadow layer style that I positioned as more of a slight outer glow.

TECHNIQUE #27

creating borders
with stock photos

*Although the main goal of this book is to create
things from scratch, don't overlook stock photography services as a source for edges, shapes, or frames.
Here, we'll use an image I found on iStockphoto.com
(some other examples appear at the end).*

key concepts:

layer masks

free transform

blend modes

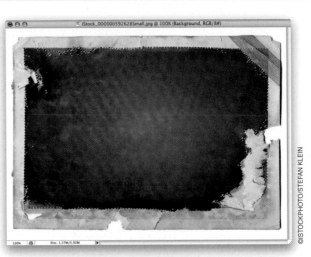

Step One:

Open the stock photo you're going to use, and
select the area(s) where you want your photo
to appear (in this case, I used the Magic Wand
tool and the Lasso tool to make my selection).

Step Two:

Switch to your photo and press Command-A
(PC: Control-A) to select the entire photo, then
Command-C (PC: Control-C) to Copy it. Switch
back to the stock photo and choose Edit>Paste
Into—a layer mask is automatically created this
way. If necessary, use Free Transform (Command-T [PC: Control-T]) to scale the pasted
photo to fit (by default the layer and layer
mask are not linked, so you can scale the photo
without affecting the layer mask).

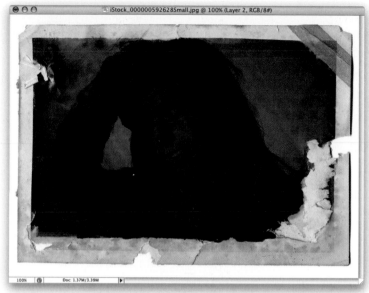

Here the photo layer's blend mode was changed to Multiply

Step Three:

For some images, the last step might be using Free Transform. In this case, due to the nature of the stock photo, a couple more steps were required. I changed the blend mode of the photo layer to Multiply using the pop-up menu at the top of the Layers palette, then duplicated the layer by pressing Command-J (PC: Control-J). Finally, the blend mode of the duplicated layer was changed to Luminosity. This helped create the look of a somewhat faded, sepia photo.

Here the duplicate layer's blend mode was changed to Luminosity

variations:

Here's another image from iStockphoto.com of an old photo border. In this case, it was a simple matter to select the black area of the stock photo and use Paste Into to add my image.

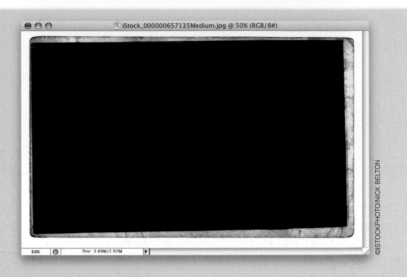

©ISTOCKPHOTO/NICK BELTON

Variation 1

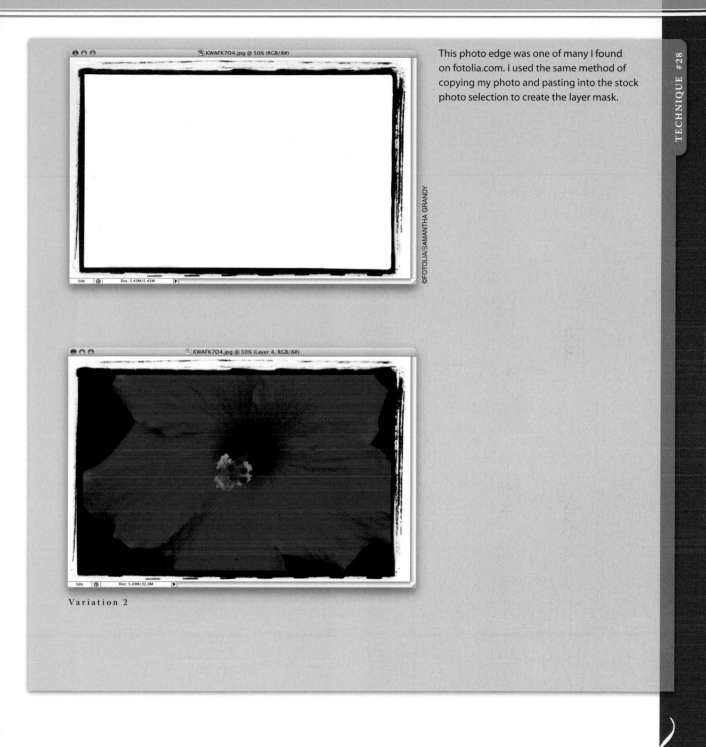

This photo edge was one of many I found on fotolia.com. I used the same method of copying my photo and pasting into the stock photo selection to create the layer mask.

©FOTOLIA/SAMANTHA GRANDY

Variation 2

Here's an iStockphoto image of an old battered Polaroid. Again, a simple Copy, Paste Into, and Free Transform and I was done.

©ISTOCKPHOTO

©STEPHANIE CROSS

Variation 3

III

color & artistic effects

Perhaps the best thing I can tell you about the techniques in this section is that they should have a warning label attached—Warning: Once you start experimenting with the many possibilities that are available to you, you may experience loss of sleep and find yourself starting every sentence with "I wonder what will happen if I try..."

The beauty of these techniques is that you're never really finished, since you can always come back and try a different setting, tweak an adjustment layer, or apply a different filter or two (or five). Of course, that's also why I think there's a need for the warning label, because you're never really finished. It can be bordering on addictive when you start digging into the unlimited options at your fingertips. Don't say I didn't warn you!

making colors pop with curves

This technique comes from what I think of as the "Photoshop trickle-down effect." Someone comes up with a technique, writes a book about it, then another Photoshop instructor reads the technique and passes it on. Scott Kelby showed me this technique from Dan Margulis' book, Photoshop LAB Color. Dan goes into much more detail and many more variations, but here I'll give you the basics of this very cool way to make your colors "pop."

key concepts:

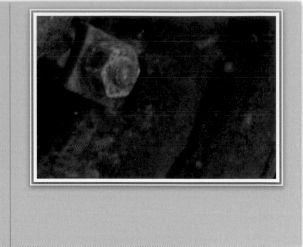

adjustment
layers

Here's the original image for this example.

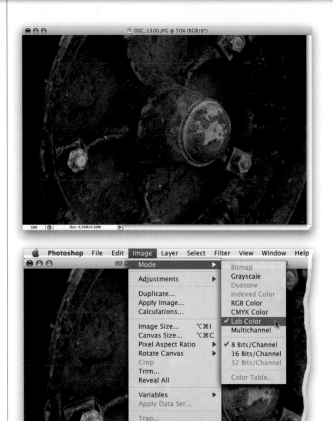

Step One:

From the Image menu, choose Mode>Lab Color to change your image into Lab Color mode. (If you look in the Channels palette you'll see channels called Lightness, "a," and "b," rather than Red, Green, and Blue as you'd see in an RGB image.)

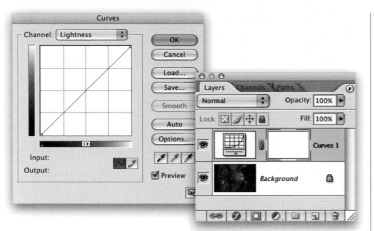

Step Two:

Click on the Create New Adjustment Layer icon at the bottom of the Layers palette to add a Curves adjustment layer to the document. (Eventually you'll probably use the Curves command, but for now I want you to be able to experiment with this technique, so we'll use an adjustment layer.) Press-and-hold the Option key (PC: Alt key) and click once on the Curves grid to make a smaller grid.

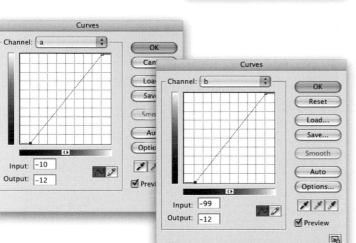

Step Three:

From the Channel pop-up menu at the top of the dialog, choose the "a" channel. Click on the top-right corner point of the curve and drag the point in to the left one square of the grid. Then click on the bottom-left corner point of the curve and drag that point in one square to the right. Now switch to the "b" channel and do the same thing.

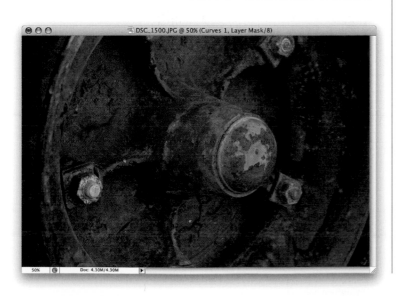

Here's the result of adjusting both the "a" and "b" channel curves in the Curves dialog.

Step Four:

As an optional step, in the Curves dialog you can choose the Lightness channel, click in the center of the curve, and drag straight up very slightly to lighten the image. Once you're finished adjusting the curves, you will change the mode back to RGB.

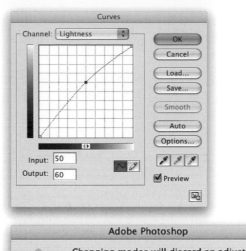

NOTE

If you have an adjustment layer in your document, you'll get a warning dialog when you switch from Lab Color to RGB, since adjustment layers cannot be included when you change modes. Your choices are to Merge, meaning make the adjustment layer permanent, Cancel, or click OK to discard the effects of the adjustment layer. Unless you aren't happy with the adjustment layer, you'll want to choose Merge.

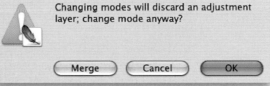

Step Five:

Since this is an operation that you may find yourself repeating over and over again, you may want to consider making it into an action. The next few steps will show you how. These are, however, entirely optional. To turn this technique into an action, first click on the Create New Set icon at the bottom of the Actions palette to create a set (folder) to contain your action, then click on the Create New Action icon, name it in the New Action dialog, and click Record.

Step Six:

Repeat the steps we've done in this technique (except we'll use the Curves command rather than an adjustment layer): Convert the mode to Lab Color; press Command-M (PC: Control-M) to open Curves; select the "a" channel and move the two ends of the curve in; select the "b" channel and move the two ends of the curve in; click OK; and convert back to RGB mode. Click on the Stop Recording icon at the bottom of the Actions palette.

Step Seven:

Once the action has been recorded, you can leave it as is so that it runs automatically with these settings, or click to the left of the Curves step in the Action, which will cause the Action to pause and open the Curves dialog for you to tweak the settings.

variations:

In the original example, I moved the "a" and "b" curves in one grid square. Depending on the image, you may want to push those curves a little further. Here's the same photo with the ends of the "a" and "b" curves moved in two grid squares.

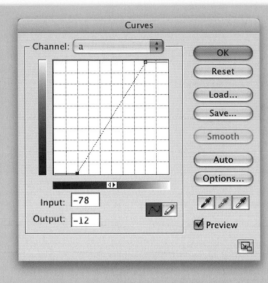

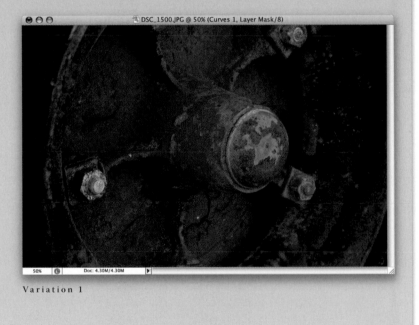

Variation 1

Here's another photo to show the effects of the Lab Curves technique.

Before

After

making colors pop with apply image

key concepts:

blend modes

In another case of passing knowledge on from the ultimate expert, here's another technique that is adapted from Dan Margulis and his Photoshop LAB Color *book. This time, we'll use the Apply Image command in Lab Color mode.*

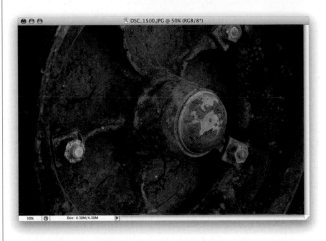

Here's the original photo.

Step One:

From the Image menu, choose Mode>Lab Color to change your image from RGB mode to Lab Color mode.

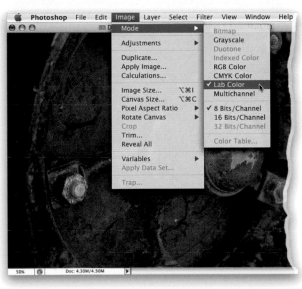

Step Two:

From the Image menu, choose Apply Image. In this dialog, you can try any number of settings, but you'll most likely be choosing between Overlay and Soft Light blend modes, and choosing between using the Lab, "a," or "b" channels (unless you're going for the "bizzaro" look, your choice will hardly ever be the Lightness channel).

Here I've created examples of each combination with the same image so you can compare (of course, with each photo the results—and therefore the choices you make—will vary).

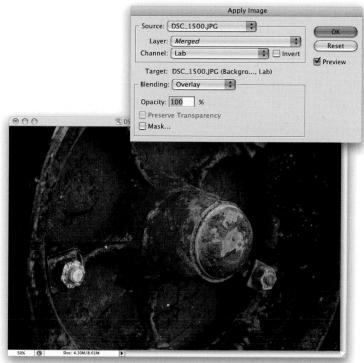

Channel: Lab; Blending: Overlay

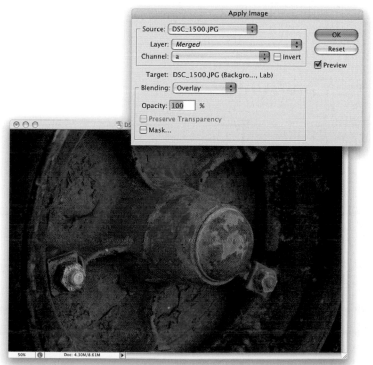

Channel: a; Blending: Overlay

In general, Soft Light will have a more subtle effect than Overlay. On the other hand, if Overlay is too much and Soft Light is not enough, try using Overlay and lowering the Opacity slightly to lessen the effect.

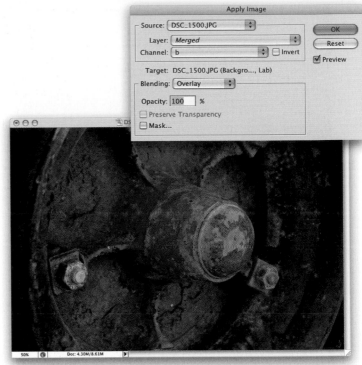

Channel: b; Blending: Overlay

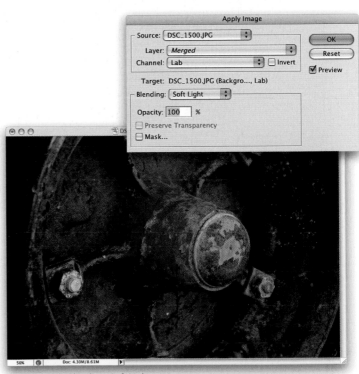

Channel: Lab; Blending: Soft Light

Another option would be to change to Lab Color mode and then duplicate the Background layer before using Apply Image—that way you can reduce the Opacity of the duplicated layer to let the original image show through.

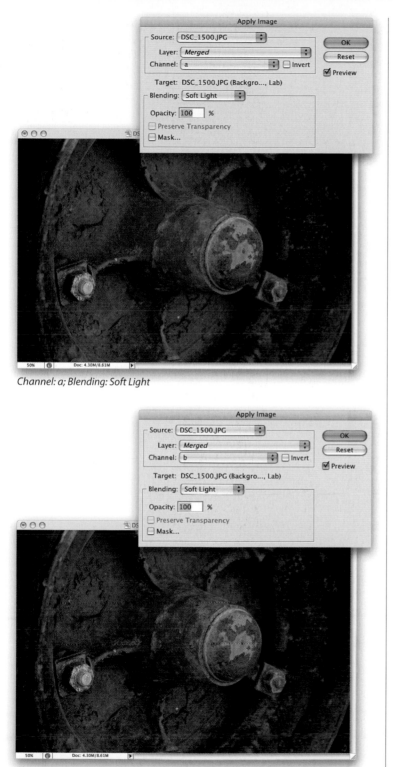

Channel: a; Blending: Soft Light

Channel: b; Blending: Soft Light

Here's another example that shows the before and after using Lab Color mode and Apply Image.

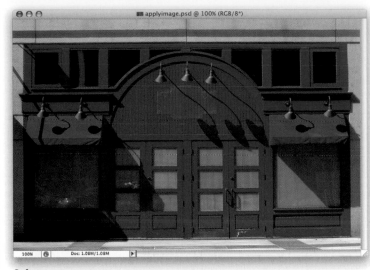

Before

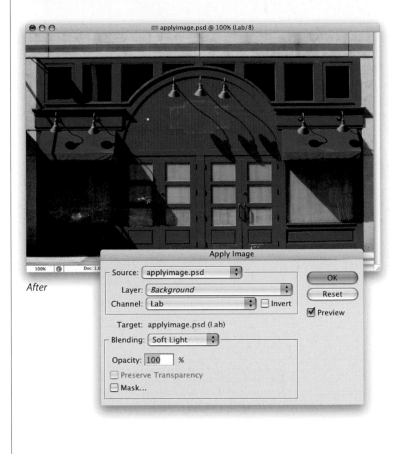

After

key concepts:

quick mask

blend modes

burned-in edges— version 1

Adding slightly darker edges to the photo— often known as burned-in edges—can help focus attention on the center of an image and add drama. In typical Photoshop fashion, there are many different ways to achieve this result. We'll look at three different methods over the next three techniques.

Here's the photo for this example (and for the next two techniques, so you can compare the results). This first method can be done very quickly, but doesn't offer a lot of flexibility should you want to tweak the results.

Step One:

Add a new layer above the Background layer by clicking on the Create a New Layer icon at the bottom of the Layers palette, and then fill the layer with black. A simple way to do this is to press D to set the Foreground and Background colors to the default, and then press Option-Delete (PC: Alt-Backspace), the shortcut for Fill with Foreground Color.

Step Two:

Using the Rectangular Marquee tool (M), click-and-drag a large selection, leaving a slight border on the photo. From the Select menu, choose Feather and enter a high value—I used 60 in this case.

> **NOTE**
>
> You can take advantage of Quick Mask mode (Q) to help determine how much to feather—see the Key Concepts section for details.

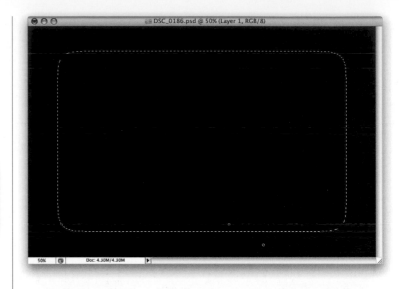

Step Three:

Press Delete (PC: Backspace) and then Command-D (PC: Control-D) to Deselect. Lower the Opacity of the black border layer and experiment with the layer blend modes, such as Multiply. Here I set the Opacity to 35% and used the Multiply blend mode.

variation:

Here, instead of adding a layer filled with black, I duplicated the Background layer by pressing Command-J (PC: Control-J), changed the layer blend mode to Multiply, and then selected and deleted the center area of the photo.

Variation 1

burned-in edges— version 2

This method of adding slightly darker edges to the photo has one distinct advantage and that is the ability to easily change the settings to try other effects—or even copy the effect to another photo.

key concepts:

adjustment layers

filters

free transform

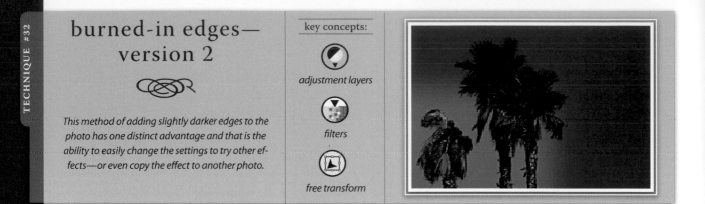

Here's the photo I'm going to start with for this example.

Step One:

Click on the Create New Adjustment Layer icon at the bottom of the Layers palette, and add a Levels adjustment layer from the pop-up menu. Pull the black Input Levels slider almost all the way to the right to darken the image. If some of the outer edges are still visible, you can also drag the white Output Levels slider to the left. (Don't worry too much about the center portion of the photo, since you'll be eliminating the effect from this area in a later step.)

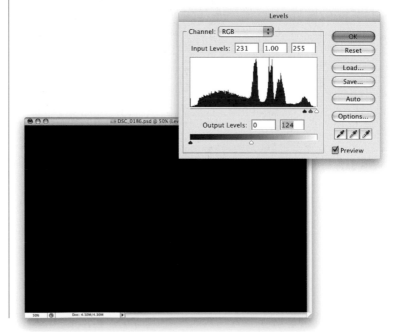

Step Two:

Using the Rectangular Marquee tool (M), make a selection that leaves a slight border around the image. Press D, then X to set the Foreground color to black, and then press Option-Delete (PC: Alt-Backspace) to fill the adjustment layer's layer mask with black. (At this point, the edges will be very sharp.)

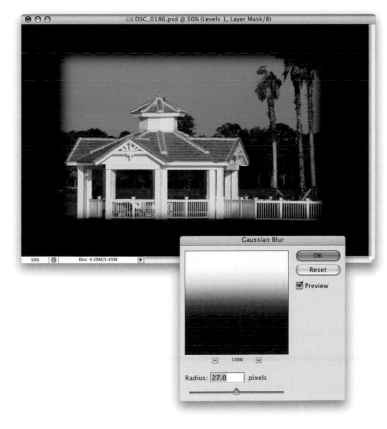

Step Three:

Press Command-D (PC: Control-D) to Deselect your rectangle, and then from the Filter menu choose Blur>Gaussian Blur. Take advantage of the preview window in the filter dialog to determine how much you want to blur the layer mask.

Step Four:

If necessary, lower the Opacity of the adjustment layer to make the effect more subtle. You can also double-click on the Levels thumbnail to tweak the settings and change the effect of the burned-in edges.

Along with the flexibility of editing the adjustment layer, one of the advantages of this technique is the ability to resize the layer mask using Free Transform, and to drag-and-drop the adjustment layer from one image to another as shown here.

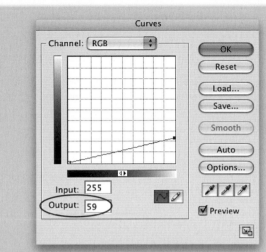

variation:

It's also possible to achieve a similar result using a Curves adjustment layer. Drag the top-right point of the curve well down the right-hand side of the grid until the Output setting is in the 50–70 range. Then follow Steps Two to Four to mask out the effects of the adjustment layer from the center of the photo.

Variation 1: Curves adjustment layer

burned-in edges— version 3

Here are a couple of options for creating a more subtle burned-in edges effect: the first using Camera Raw, and the second using the Lens Correction filter.

key concepts:

layer masks

filters

For this first technique, you must use a RAW file.

Step One:

Double-click on the RAW file to open it in Camera Raw. Choose the image size you want from the Size pop-up menu underneath the preview window, and click Open to create the original photo.

Step Two:

Double-click on the RAW file again to open it in Camera Raw once more. Keep all other settings the same, click on the Lens tab on the right side of the dialog, and then drag the Vignetting Amount slider to the left to darken the outer edges of the photo. You can also experiment with the Vignetting Midpoint slider. Click Open.

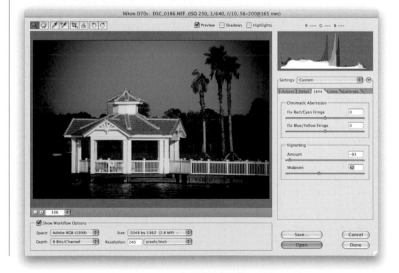

Step Three:

Using the Move tool (V), with the Shift key held down, click-and-drag the second copy of the image (with the burned-in edges) onto the original photo.

Step Four:

If you want the effect to be even more subtle, add a layer mask to the top layer by clicking on the Add Layer Mask icon at the bottom of the Layers palette. With the layer mask active, use the Rectangular Marquee tool (M) to create a large selection that leaves a slight border. Fill the selection with black by pressing D, then X to set your Foreground color to black, then pressing Option-Delete (PC: Alt-Backspace). Use the Gaussian Blur filter (Filter>Blur>Gaussian Blur) to soften the edges of the layer mask.

You can also apply a similar effect to JPEG files by using the Lens Correction filter, as you'll see in the following steps.

Step One:

Press Command-J (PC: Control-J) to duplicate the Background layer.

Step Two:

From the Filter menu, choose Distort>Lens Correction. In the Lens Correction dialog, you may want to hide the grid by turning off the Show Grid checkbox below the preview window. Drag the Vignette Amount slider to the left to darken the outer edges of the photo. You can also experiment with the Vignette Midpoint slider.

The final result is shown here.

Step Three:

If you want the effect to be even more subtle, add a layer mask to the top layer by clicking on the Add Layer Mask icon at the bottom of the Layers palette. With the layer mask active, use the Rectangular Marquee tool (M) to create a large selection that leaves a slight border. Fill the selection with black by pressing D, then X to set your Foreground color to black, then pressing Option-Delete (PC: Alt-Backspace). Use the Gaussian Blur filter (Filter>Blur>Gaussian Blur) to soften the edges of the layer mask.

spotlight effect

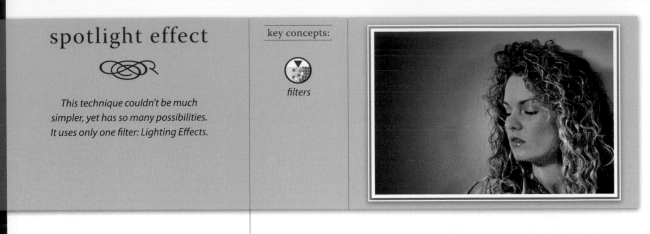

This technique couldn't be much simpler, yet has so many possibilities. It uses only one filter: Lighting Effects.

key concepts:

filters

Step One:

Press Command-J (PC: Control-J) to duplicate the Background layer.

Step Two:

From the Filter menu, choose Render>Lighting Effects. There are a ton of options in the dialog (almost an overwhelming amount), but we're only going to change one setting: change the Style to Flashlight. Make sure the Preview checkbox on the left side of the dialog is turned on. Then, in the preview window, click-and-drag on the center dot of the lighting circle to change its position, and click-and-drag on the handles on the circle to change its size. Although you can also experiment with the Properties settings, for this time, just click OK.

That's it! In only two steps, you've added a pretty nice dramatic lighting effect. Since you applied the filter to a copy of the Background layer, you can lower the opacity of the top layer to lessen the effect (not shown).

variations:

Here, I changed the blend mode of the filtered layer to Multiply.

In this case, I put the blend mode back to Normal and noticed that the filter introduced a slight hot spot on her face, so I added a layer mask (by clicking on the Add Layer Mask icon at the bottom of the Layers palette) and used the Brush tool (B) to paint on it with black to hide that area of the filtered photo, eliminating the hot spot.

Variation 1

Variation 2

Here, the filtered layer was duplicated and its blend mode changed to Multiply, with the opacity lowered to 60%.

In this example, I added a Hue/Saturation adjustment layer, turned on the Colorize checkbox at the bottom right of the dialog, and experimented with the Hue slider.

Variation 3

Variation 4

Of course, this doesn't only work with portraits!
Here's a before and after of another photo
where I used this same Flashlight lighting effect
(and used a layer mask to lessen the effects of
the filter in the edges of the flower).

Before adding the spotlight effect

After adding the spotlight effect

202

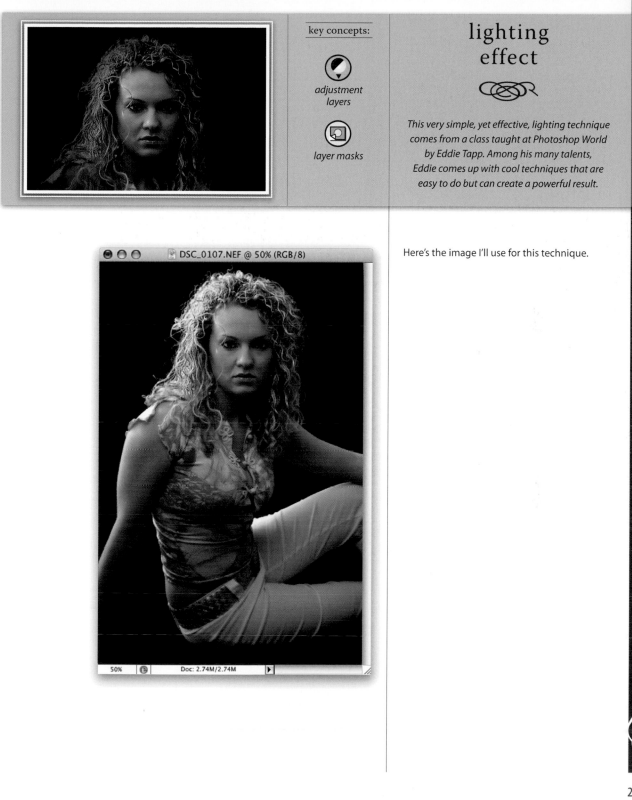

key concepts:

adjustment layers

layer masks

lighting effect

This very simple, yet effective, lighting technique comes from a class taught at Photoshop World by Eddie Tapp. Among his many talents, Eddie comes up with cool techniques that are easy to do but can create a powerful result.

Here's the image I'll use for this technique.

DSC_0107.NEF @ 50% (RGB/8)

50%   Doc: 2.74M/2.74M

Step One:

Click on the Create New Adjustment Layer icon at the bottom of the Layers palette, and add a Curves adjustment layer from the pop-up menu. Click on the top-right point of the curve and drag it straight down until the Output number is between 70 and 100.

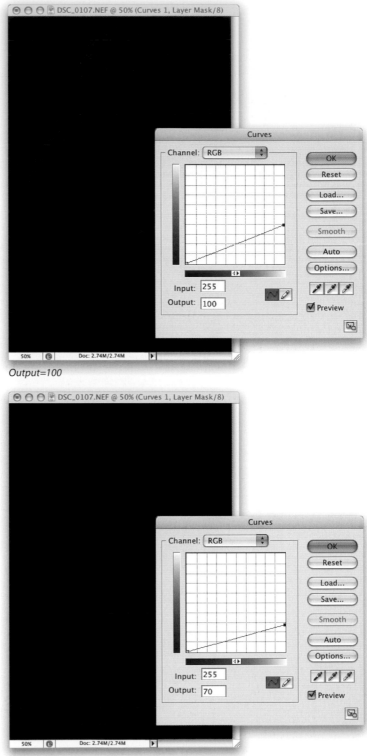

Output=100

Output=70

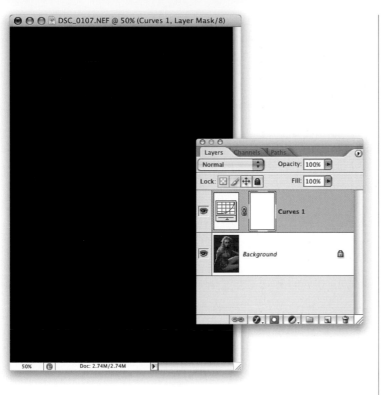

Here's the result of my Curves adjustment layer.

Step Two:

Press B to get the Brush tool and choose a very large, soft-edged brush. Make sure your Foreground is set to black and, in the Options Bar, set the Opacity of the brush to around 50–60%. Click once on the image to hide the effects of the adjustment layer (and add the lighting effect). In this example, I then changed the brush opacity to 20%, moved the position of the brush slightly, and clicked again. Here's the result and what my layer mask looked like.

variations:

Here, I changed the blend mode of the adjustment layer to Multiply, which intensifies the darker areas.

Variation 1: Multiply

Rather than using a brush to mask the effects of the Curves adjustment layer, you can also use a selection. Here, I used the Lasso tool (L) to make a rough selection of the area I wanted to light, and pressed Option-Delete (PC: Alt-Backspace) to fill it with black. After deselecting, I used Filter>Blur>Gaussian Blur to create the look I wanted by experimenting with different amounts of blurring.

Variation 2: Selection and Gaussian Blur

TECHNIQUE #36

gritty extreme-contrast effect—version 1

This seems to be a pretty trendy effect—taking a photo and giving it a very "gritty" look with lots of contrast. We'll be able to produce a range of possibilities without having to actually alter the Background layer.

key concepts:

filters

blend modes

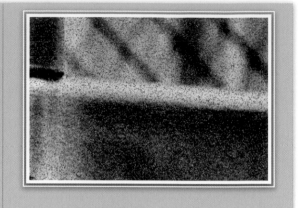

This is our starting image.

Step One:

Press Command-J (PC: Control-J) to duplicate the Background layer.

Step Two:

From the Filter menu, choose Other>High Pass. In the dialog, move the slider or enter a value in the Radius field, aiming to create an image that has only a slight gray look to it. Compare the two settings shown here. A value of 4 pixels still has a lot of gray in the image. This will not create the high-contrast look we want (but after changing the blend mode to Hard Light as we will in the next step, this setting in the High Pass filter does a nicer job sharpening the photo). Using a setting of 32 pixels introduces some areas of higher contrast and has a little less gray in it.

Step Three:

Change the blend mode of the top (filtered) layer to Hard Light (Overlay will provide similar but slightly different results, depending on the photo).

If you want an even more intense effect, press Command-J (PC: Control-J) to duplicate the filtered layer. This will double-up the effect of the filter.

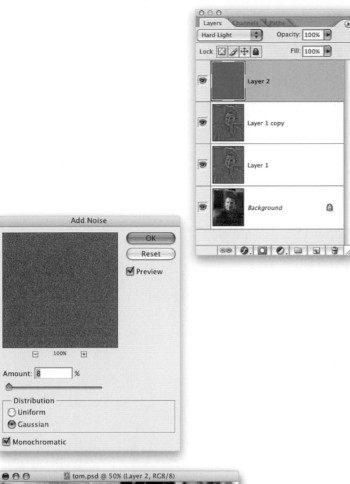

Step Four:

Add a new layer at the top of the layer stack by clicking on the Create a New Layer icon at the bottom of the Layers palette, and fill it with 50% gray (the Edit>Fill command has 50% Gray as a built-in choice). Change the blend mode of this layer to Hard Light.

Step Five:

From the Filter menu, choose Noise>Add Noise, and in the filter dialog, change the Amount to somewhere in the 5–10% range (as always, this will vary with the resolution of your image and the look of the image itself). In the dialog's preview window, you'll see the noise being added to the gray layer, but if you look at the document, you'll see how the filter is affecting the photo.

variations:

In this example, I duplicated the Background layer and then used the Unsharp Mask filter with very high settings. Then I duplicated that layer and used the High Pass filter and Hard Light blend mode as described earlier.

Variation 1

tom.psd @ 50% (Hue/Saturation 1, Layer Mask/8)

50%   Doc: 2.99M/19.4M

Variation 2

Here, I added a Hue/Saturation adjustment layer at the top of the layer stack (by clicking on the Create New Adjustment Layer icon at the bottom of the Layers palette and choosing Hue/Saturation) and dropped the Saturation slider to -45 to remove some of the color.

gritty extreme-contrast effect—version 2

This version of the high-contrast/gritty look relies on using one or more channels to give us a head start.

key concepts:

blend modes

filters

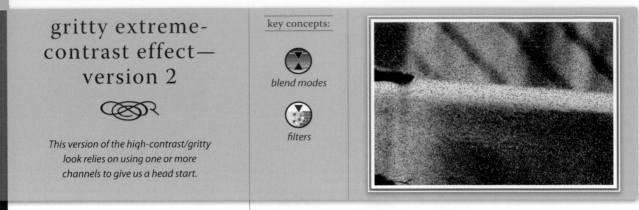

Here's the original photo.

Step One:

In the Channels palette (nested behind the Layers palette by default), look at the Red, Green, and Blue channels to find the one that has the most contrast in the key area of the photo (in this case, I'm looking for the most contrast in his face). Very often it will be the Green or Blue channel—in this photo the Blue channel gives the most contrast.

Step Two:

Click-and-drag the Blue channel onto the Create New Channel icon at the bottom of the palette to duplicate the channel. The new channel will be called "Blue copy" (unless, of course, you duplicate the Green channel, making the name "Green copy").

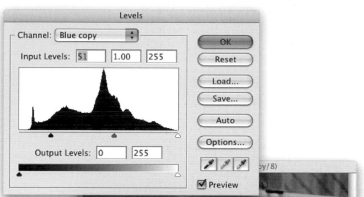

Step Three:

With the copied channel still active, press Command-L (PC: Control-L) to open the Levels dialog. Drag the black Input Levels slider to the right to darken the image.

Optional:

With the copied channel still active, from the Image menu, choose Apply Image. Select Blue copy as the channel and Soft Light from the Blending pop-up menu. This will darken up the channel just a little more.

Step Four:

Click on the RGB Composite channel and then go to the Layers palette. Press Command-J (PC: Control-J) to duplicate the Background layer.

Step Five:

From the Image menu, choose Apply Image, and choose Blue copy as the channel. In the Blending pop-up menu, choose from the blend modes shown here to get slightly different results. You can also try tweaking the Opacity setting.

Blending: Hard Light; Opacity: 90%

Blending: Overlay; Opacity: 100%

Blending: Multiply; Opacity: 70%

Step Six:

Add a new layer on top of the layer stack by clicking on the Create a New Layer icon at the bottom of the Layers palette, and fill it with 50% gray (using Edit>Fill, where 50% Gray is a built-in choice). Change the layer blend mode of this gray layer to Hard Light.

Step Seven:

From the Filter menu, choose Noise>Add Noise. Turn on the Monochromatic checkbox and experiment with fairly low numbers to add a little noise to the image.

variation:

If the detail gets lost a little too much in some areas (like his eyes, in this example), Command-click (PC: Control-click) on all the layers except the Background layer to select them, and press Command-G (PC: Control-G) to put the layers into a Group. Then, click on the Add Layer Mask icon to add a layer mask to the Group and use the Brush tool (B) to paint with 50% black to slightly hide the effects around the eyes.

Variation 1

key concepts:

filters

blend modes

layer masks

high-contrast fashion look

Here's another popular effect that's often used to create a high-fashion, high-contrast look. It tends to work best with portraits, but of course, you could try this effect on many different types of photos.

Here's the original image I used.

Step One:

Press Command-J (PC: Control-J) to duplicate the Background layer.

Step Two:

Choose the color you want to use for the Diffuse Glow filter and make that color your Background color (yes, I said Background not Foreground). In general, you'll probably want to use white, or a very light color chosen from the image. Once your Background color is chosen, go to Filter>Distort>Diffuse Glow. As always, feel free to play with the numbers here, but I'd suggest starting with a pretty low value for Graininess and fairly high numbers for Glow Amount and Clear Amount. Click OK.

Step Three:

If the effect is too pronounced, lower the opacity of the layer (I used 70% in this example).

If you want to bring back the original colors just a little more, try changing the layer blend mode to Luminosity and lowering the opacity slightly.

Step Four:

You could stop after the Diffuse Glow filter, or add a little more of a bright highlight in the next two steps. Click on the Background layer to activate it and from the Select menu, choose Color Range. From the Select pop-up menu in the Color Range dialog, choose Highlights, then click the Selection radio button at the bottom, and click OK. This will select all the highlights in the image.

Step Five:

Add a new layer at the top of the layer stack by clicking on the top layer, then clicking on the Create a New Layer icon at the bottom of the Layers palette. Press D to set your Foreground and Background to the default colors, and press Command-Delete (PC: Control-Back-space) to fill the selection with white. Press Command-D (PC: Control-D) to Deselect. Lower the layer's opacity until the effect is not quite so obvious (I used 45%, in my example).

Again, you could stop there or, if you like, bring back a little bit of the shadow details in key areas such as eyes and lips (assuming of course, you're working with a portrait). To do this, Command-click (PC: Control-click) on the two layers above the Background layer to select them and press Command-G (PC: Control-G) to put them into a Group. Then, click on the Add Layer Mask icon at the bottom of the Layers palette to add a layer mask to the Group. Using the Brush tool (B), choose a soft-edged brush from the Brush Picker, set the Opacity to 20–30% in the Options Bar, and with black as the Foreground color, paint over the shadow and detail areas.

variations:

To create a slight color tint, I added a Solid Color adjustment layer above the Background layer (by clicking on the Create New Adjustment Layer icon at the bottom of the Layers palette), chose the color I wanted, changed the layer blend mode to Color and lowered the Opacity to 70%.

Variation 1: Solid Color adjustment layer

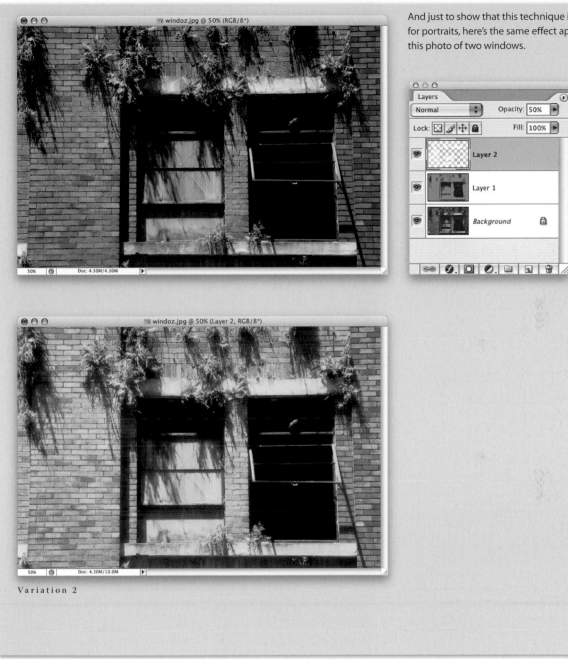

And just to show that this technique is not only for portraits, here's the same effect applied to this photo of two windows.

Variation 2

convert to black & white— version 1

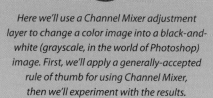

Here we'll use a Channel Mixer adjustment layer to change a color image into a black-and-white (grayscale, in the world of Photoshop) image. First, we'll apply a generally-accepted rule of thumb for using Channel Mixer, then we'll experiment with the results.

key concepts:

adjustment layers

Here's the image I'll use in this technique.

©STEPHANIE CROSS

Step One:

Click on the Create New Adjustment Layer icon at the bottom of the Layers palette, and from the pop-up menu, choose Channel Mixer. By default it will display the Red channel at 100% and the others at 0%. Turn on the Monochrome checkbox and start experimenting with the three Source Channels sliders. The rule of thumb that works well for many images is to aim to have the three numbers add up to roughly 100.

You can experiment with a variety of combinations, but be careful to avoid blowing out any areas of the photo (unless you want that to happen). In this example, the settings for the three channels were quite different but still added up to around the 100 mark.

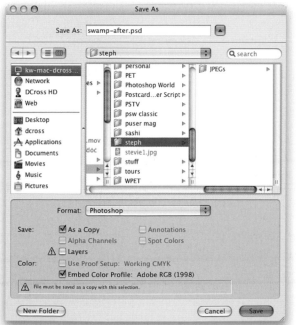

Step Two:

Okay, so there really isn't a Step Two, unless you consider clicking OK a step. At this point, the Channel Mixer is making the photo appear in black and white, but we're still in RGB mode. I would recommend saving your document as is (in RGB with the adjustment layer), then using Save As to create a copy, flattening the layers and changing the mode (to Grayscale) of the copy. That way, you still have the original with an adjustment layer that you can tweak at any time.

variations:

In this example, I added a Gradient Map adjustment layer (above the Channel Mixer adjustment layer), using a simple black-to-white gradient.

Variation 1: Black-to-white Gradient Map adjustment layer

Here I changed the blend mode of the Gradient Map adjustment layer to Luminosity.

Variation 2: Luminosity Gradient Map adjustment layer

This time I changed the blend mode of the Channel Mixer adjustment layer to Hue.

Variation 3: Hue Channel Mixer adjustment layer

In order to fade the effects of the two adjustment layers (to make the photo have a slight color tint), I selected both layers and, from the Layers palette's flyout menu, chose New Group from Layers. Then I lowered the Opacity of the Group (folder) in the resulting dialog to 75%.

Variation 4: Faded adjustment layers

convert to black & white— version 2

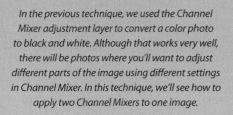

In the previous technique, we used the Channel Mixer adjustment layer to convert a color photo to black and white. Although that works very well, there will be photos where you'll want to adjust different parts of the image using different settings in Channel Mixer. In this technique, we'll see how to apply two Channel Mixers to one image.

 key concepts:

adjustment layers

layer masks

Here's the photo I'll use.

Step One:

Click on the Create New Adjustment Layer icon at the bottom of the Layers palette, and from the pop-up menu, choose Channel Mixer. Turn on the Monochrome checkbox and start experimenting with the three sliders, making sure that the focal point of the image (in this case, the buildings) looks the way you want.

Step Two:

Hide the adjustment layer by clicking on the Eye icon to the left of the layer thumbnail, then click on the Background layer and add another Channel Mixer adjustment layer. Turn on the Monochrome checkbox and move the sliders, this time focusing your attention on the remainder of the image (in my example, the sky). Don't worry if the other parts of the photo start to look poor (like the curved building in my photo).

Step Three:

The layer mask of the adjustment layer should be active but if it isn't, click on it to activate it, and then press Command-I (PC: Control-I) to Invert the mask to completely hide the effects of the adjustment layer. (Since you previously hid the other adjustment layer, your image will temporarily be in color again.)

Step Four:

Using your favorite selection tool, select the area of the photo that you want to be affected by the second Channel Mixer. In my example, I used mostly the Polygonal Lasso tool (nested with the Lasso tool) to select around the building so that I had the sky selected. Fill the selection on the layer mask with white (by pressing Option-Delete [PC: Alt-Backspace]) to show the adjustment layer in the selected area. Press Command-D (PC: Control-D) to Deselect.

Step Five:

Make the original Channel Mixer adjustment layer visible by clicking on the empty box to the left of the adjustment layer's thumbnail. Click on the layer mask for this original Channel Mixer adjustment layer to make it active. Then, Command-click (PC: Control-click) on the sky adjustment layer's mask to reload your sky selection, and press Command-Delete (PC: Control-Backspace) to fill the selection with black on the top layer mask. Press Command-D to Deselect. Now you'll have two adjustment layers, each affecting different areas of the photo (the top one affects only the buildings, while the bottom one only affects the sky).

Variation 1: Gradient added to sky layer mask

variation:

I wanted the Channel Mixer for the sky to have a more gradual effect, so I did these steps: I clicked on the layer mask for that layer to make it active, then Command-clicked (PC: Control-clicked) on the layer mask to load a selection of the sky. Then, with the Gradient tool (G), I dragged from the top to the bottom to make the effects of the adjustment layer more pronounced at the bottom and less obvious at the top.

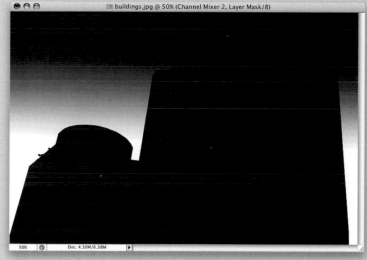

The layer mask

convert to black & white— version 3

key concepts:

adjustment layers

Katrin Eismann showed a technique at Photoshop World in her awesome class "From Color to Black and White and Back Again" that used a Hue/Saturation and a Selective Color adjustment layer to convert a color image to black and white. I thought it was a great concept and adapted it slightly here, using a Hue/Saturation and a Color Balance adjustment layer.

Here's the original image I used for this technique.

Step One:

Click on the Create New Adjustment Layer icon at the bottom of the Layers palette, and from the pop-up menu, choose Hue/Saturation. Drag the Saturation slider all the way to the left to remove all the color from the image. Click OK.

Step Two:

Click on the Background layer, and then from the Create New Adjustment Layer pop-up menu, choose Color Balance. Use the radio buttons at the bottom of the dialog to determine which range of tones you want to work on—here I started with Shadows. Then, drag the color sliders to mix in different colors (this is definitely a case of trial and error).

Step Three:

Now click on a different radio button (Highlights, in this example) and again move the color sliders. Then experiment with changing the color sliders with the Midtones radio button selected, and click OK.

One of the potential disadvantages of using Channel Mixer—that this method solves—is that it's very easy to blow out areas of the photo as you move the Channel Mixer sliders. By combining the Hue/Saturation and Color Balance adjustment layers, it's much easier to get the results you want, without as much worry about introducing blown-out areas (or said a different way, using this method, it's much harder to blow out details).

variations:

Here I changed the blend mode of the Color Balance adjustment layer to Luminosity.

One of the variations that Katrin mentioned in her class was to use a Selective Color adjustment layer with the Hue/Saturation layer. Here I used Layer>Change Layer Content to change the Color Balance layer to a Selective Color layer. Then I experimented with the different choices under the Colors pop-up menu and moved the color sliders in the Selective Color Options dialog.

Variation 1: Luminosity blend mode

Variation 2: Selective Color adjustment layer

Here, I wanted to create an image that gradually changed from color to black and white, so I selected the two adjustment layers and used the Layers palette's flyout menu to choose New Group from Layers. Then I added a layer mask to the Group (by clicking on the Add Layer Mask icon at the bottom of the Layers palette) and applied a black-to-white gradient with the Gradient tool (G).

Variation 3: Gradient added to adjustment layers

mostly black & white with a touch of color

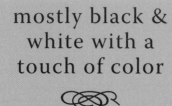

This technique shows color in just some portions of a photo while the remainder is black and white (or colorized).

key concepts:

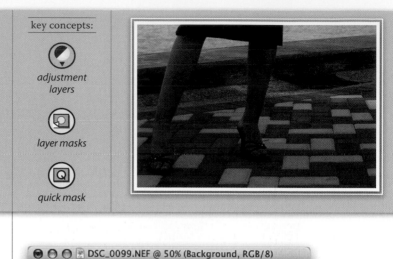

adjustment layers

layer masks

quick mask

Here's the original image.

DSC_0099.NEF @ 50% (Background, RGB/8)

50%   Doc: 2.74M/3.43M

Step One:

Start by clicking on the Create New Adjustment Layer icon at the bottom of the Layers palette, and from the pop-up menu, choose Hue/Saturation. Move the Saturation slider all the way to the left to remove all the color. If the image looks a little too dark, adjust the Lightness slider slightly to the right.

Step Two:

Now you'll need to mask the portions of the photo that you don't want to be desaturated (in other words, the areas you want to be in color). You can use the Brush tool (B) with a black brush and/or make a selection and fill it with black. Make sure the layer mask is active before you paint or fill your selection. To fill your selection, simply press D, then X to set your Foreground color to black, and press Option-Delete (PC: Alt-Backspace) to fill the selection. In this example, I did a little of both to end up with a layer mask that hid the effects of the adjustment layer and made Sabrina appear in color.

> **TIP**
>
> To see the effects of the mask as a Quick Mask, Option-click (PC: Alt-click) on the layer mask to view the mask, then press ~ (the Tilde key, at the top left of your keyboard) to view the mask as a colored overlay. Continue to paint with black and white, but use this overlay as a guide to areas that need to be tweaked. Option-click on the mask again to return to your image.

Step Three:

Since I already had gone to the trouble of creating a layer mask, I thought I'd take advantage
of it to make the colors a little more saturated.
To do this, I duplicated the Hue/Saturation
adjustment layer by pressing Command-J (PC:
Control-J) and double-clicked on the thumbnail to edit the adjustment, where I moved
the Saturation slider to the right. Initially, that
affected the background around Sabrina, so I
pressed Command-I (PC: Control-I) to Invert the
layer mask.

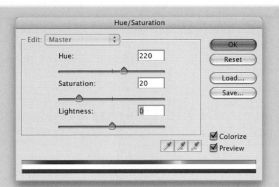

variations:

In this example, I duplicated the original Hue/Saturation adjustment layer again, and clicked-and-dragged it above the second Hue/Saturation adjustment layer. Then, I double-clicked on the thumbnail to edit the settings. In the dialog, I turned on the Colorize checkbox and moved the Hue and Saturation sliders to colorize the background of the photo.

Variation 1: Colorized background

Here, I selected the three adjustment layers and pressed Command-G (PC: Control-G) to put the layers into a Group. Then I added a layer mask to the Group and used the Gradient tool (G) to paint on the mask and gradually fade in the effects of the adjustment layers. After painting the gradient, I decided to turn off the top adjustment layer to make the background fade from color to black and white.

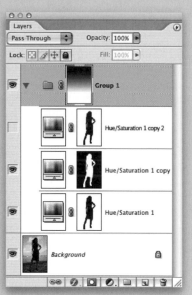

Variation 2: Gradient added to adjustments

key concepts:

adjustment
layers

blend modes

blending options

color tint— version 1

Here we'll use adjustment layers and blending options to add a color tint to a photo, with the added advantage of being able to apply a similar look to another photo just by dragging-and-dropping layers.

Here's the original image I used.

Step One:

Start by clicking on the Create New Adjustment Layer icon at the bottom of the Layers palette and, from the pop-up menu, choose Hue/Saturation. Turn on the Colorize checkbox in the Hue/Saturation dialog, and move the sliders to get the color tint you want (here, I used a Hue setting of 44 with a Saturation of 47).

245

Step Two:

To get something a little different, choosing a different layer blend mode (other than Normal) will have an effect on how the color tint appears.

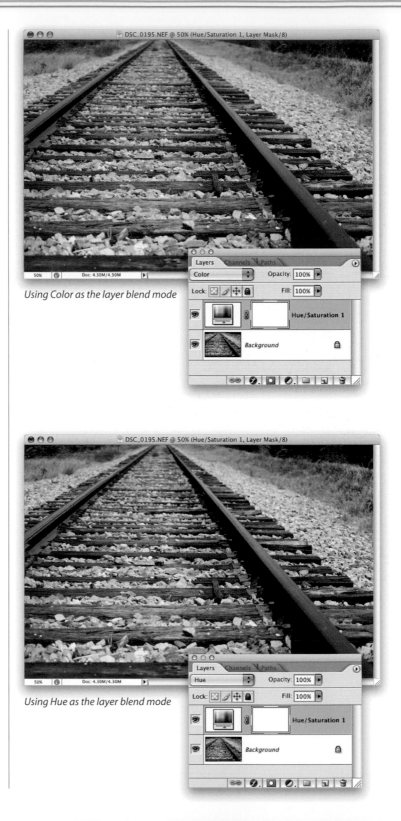

Using Color as the layer blend mode

Using Hue as the layer blend mode

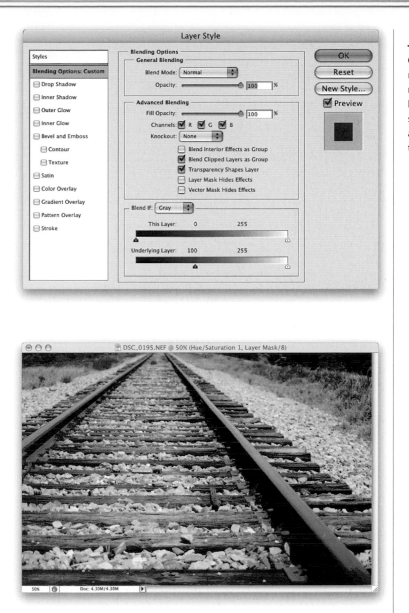

Step Three:

Control-click (PC: Right-click) on the Hue/Saturation adjustment layer and in the contextual menu, choose Blending Options. At the very bottom of the dialog, drag the black Blend If slider for the Underlying Layer to the right to allow the Background layer to show through the adjustment layer. Don't click OK yet.

Step Four:

It's quite likely that there will be areas where the transition between the adjustment layer and the Background is a little harsh (see the railroad track in the bottom-right corner). If this happens, press-and-hold the Option key (PC: Alt key) and click-and-drag on the black slider to split it in two. Drag the left half of the slider back to the left and the right half a little more to the right—this will soften the transition between the two layers. Click OK when you are done.

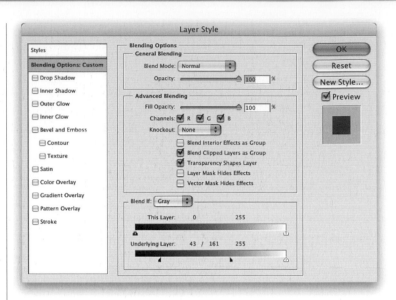

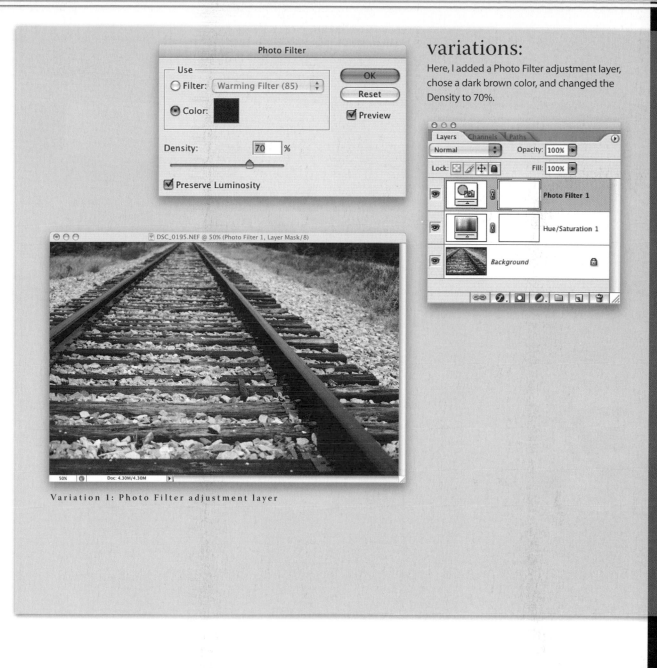

variations:

Here, I added a Photo Filter adjustment layer, chose a dark brown color, and changed the Density to 70%.

Variation 1: Photo Filter adjustment layer

One of the advantages of using adjustment layers is that you can easily apply the effect to a different photo. Here's a different photo of the railroad tracks, showing the original photo, and the result after I clicked-and-dragged both adjustment layers over from the first photo.

Variation 2

key concepts:

adjustment layers

blend modes

color tint— version 2

Here we'll use a Solid Color adjustment layer and different blend modes to experiment with tinting a photo.

My original shot looks like this.

Step One:

Click on the Create New Adjustment Layer icon at the bottom of the Layers palette, and from the pop-up menu, choose Solid Color. Pick the color you want from the Color Picker. (Initially, the layer will cover up the photo but we'll fix that next.)

Color Picker

Pick a solid color:

OK
Cancel
Color Libraries

H: 198 °   L: 64
S: 83 %   a: -40
B: 91 %   b: -45

R: 39   C: 90 %
G: 175   M: 1 %
B: 232   Y: 2 %
         K: 0 %

27afe8

☐ Only Web Colors

251

Step Two:

Change the layer blend mode to…actually I can't tell you which one to use because it will depend on your image and the look you're going for. Here are the results of some of the more common choices for blend modes.

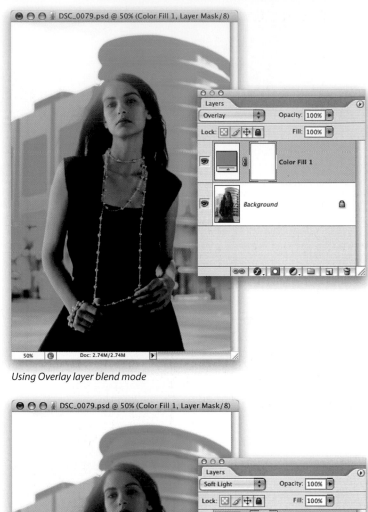

Using Overlay layer blend mode

Using Soft Light layer blend mode

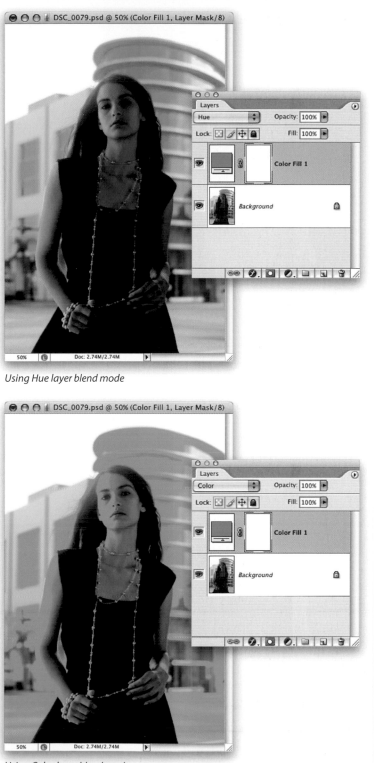

Using Hue layer blend mode

Using Color layer blend mode

Using Color layer blend mode at 50% opacity

One of the advantages of using a Solid Color adjustment layer is that at any time you can double-click on the layer thumbnail to open the Color Picker and choose a new color. As you choose a color, the results can be seen immediately on the photo.

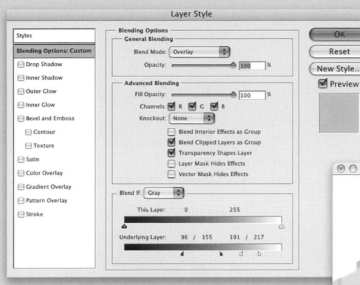

variations:

In this example, I Control-clicked (PC: Right-clicked) on the adjustment layer to access the Blending Options and then played with the Underlying Layer Blend If sliders to allow portions of the original colors to show through. (Check out the Blending Options section in Key Concepts for more information about these sliders.)

Variation 1

Here, I added a Channel Mixer adjustment layer and moved the Source Channels sliders in each of the Output Channels in the pop-up menu at the top of the dialog (with no real plan in mind, I just dragged sliders until I liked what I saw. Seriously). Then I changed the blend mode of the Channel Mixer layer to Color.

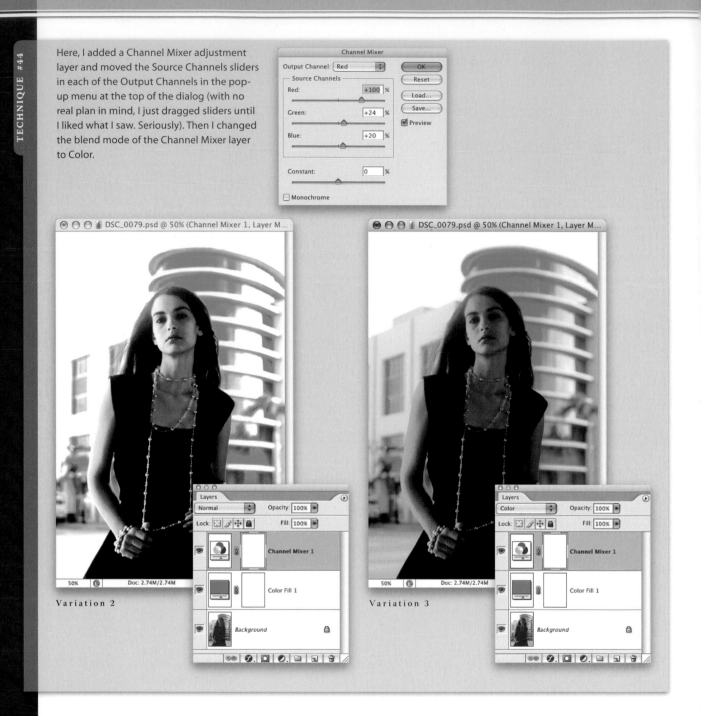

Variation 2

Variation 3

After selecting both adjustment layers, I pressed Command-G (PC: Control-G) to put them into a Group, added a layer mask, pressed G to get the Gradient tool, and used a Radial gradient (the second icon from the left in the Options Bar) to hide the effects of the adjustments around her face.

Variation 4

make it old

This technique starts with a color tint (Technique #43) and adds to it to make the photo look old. As with many of the techniques, this one uses separate layers that can easily be copied to other photos.

key concepts:

adjustment layers

filters

blend modes

layers masks

Step One:

Follow the steps in Technique #43 to add a color tint to the photo—a sepia kind of look lends itself well to the old-fashioned look. All the layers we'll add will be below the two adjustment layers.

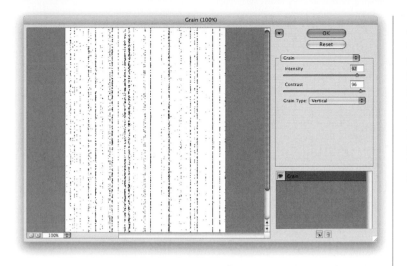

Step Two:

Click on the Background layer and then click on the Create a New Layer icon at the bottom of the Layers palette to add a new layer above the Background layer. Fill it with white by pressing D to set your Foreground and Background colors to the default, then pressing Command-Delete (PC: Control-Backspace). From the Filter menu, choose Texture>Grain. Change the Grain Type to Vertical and put in high values (I used 92 for Intensity and 96 for Contrast).

Step Three:

Change the blend mode of the grain layer to Multiply to force the white areas to disappear. If the lines created by the filter are not to your liking, try re-applying the filter to the same layer.

Step Four:

To randomize the lines a little, click the Add Layer Mask icon at the bottom of the Layers palette to add a mask to the grain layer. From the Filter menu, choose Render>Clouds. Press Command-F (PC: Control-F) to create a different cloud pattern to mask the grain layer slightly differently.

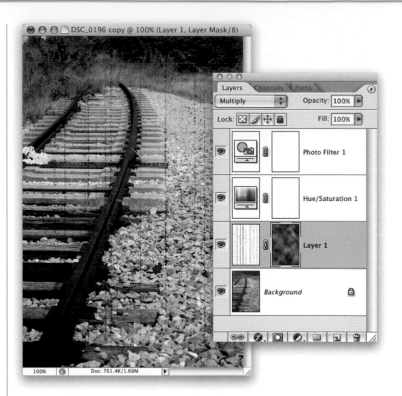

Step Five:

Add a Levels adjustment layer and click-and-drag the white Input Levels slider to the left to over-brighten the photo. Click OK and then press Command-I (PC: Control-I) to Invert the layer mask and hide the effects of the Levels adjustment.

Step Six:

With white as the Foreground color and black as the Background color (press D to set these), click on the Gradient tool (G) and in the Options Bar, change to the Radial gradient (the second icon from the left). Press Return (PC: Enter) to bring up the Gradient Picker and choose the Foreground to Background gradient (in the top left). Press Return again to close the Picker. Change the tool's blend mode to Screen. Position the cursor close to one corner of the photo and then click-and-drag a short distance. Repeat in another corner (or other area) of the photo.

As an optional step, you can experiment with applying filters to the layer mask, such as Artistic>Plastic Wrap, as shown here.

Step Seven:

Add a new layer and fill it with 50% gray (use Edit>Fill, where 50% Gray is a built-in option). From the Filter menu, choose Noise>Add Noise, turn on the Monochromatic checkbox and use a low setting. Change the blend mode of the noise layer to Hard Light.

Step Eight:

As we did in Step Four, add a layer mask to the noise layer and use the Filter>Render> Clouds command to randomize the visibility of the noise.

Before

One of the advantages of using separate layers is the option to select them all and drag them onto a different photo—as long as the other photo is relatively close to the same size. Here's the result of clicking-and-dragging the layers used in this technique onto a second photo.

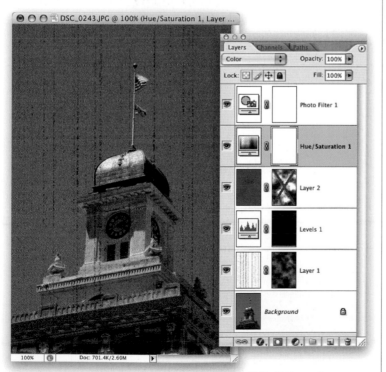

After: The layer mask on the grain layer was disabled by Shift-clicking on it

gradient map

With just the addition of a Gradient Map adjustment layer, you can add all kinds of color effects to your image, as I'll show you here.

key concepts:

adjustment
layers

Here's the original image.

Step One:

Click on the Create New Adjustment Layer icon at the bottom of the Layers palette, and from the pop-up menu, choose Gradient Map. In the Gradient Map dialog, click on the down-facing triangle next to the gradient thumbnail to get the Gradient Picker. If black and white are not your current Foreground and Background colors, choose the third (Black, White) gradient from the left in the top row, otherwise you can use the Foreground to Background gradient in the top left.

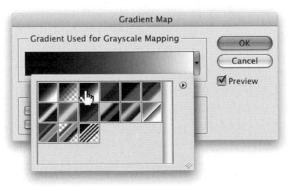

This will add a black-and-white effect to your color photo, as you can see here.

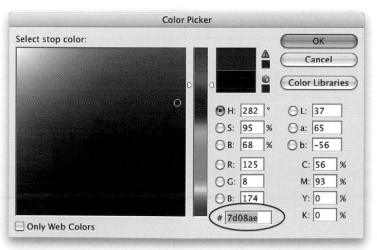

Step Two:

If you clicked OK, double-click on the adjustment layer's thumbnail to reopen the Gradient Map dIalog, then click once on the gradient thumbnail itself (not the triangle) to open the Gradient Editor.

Step Three:

In the bottom half of the Gradient Editor, double-click on the first (far left) black color stop to choose the main color you want to use. In the resulting Color Picker, after choosing your color, highlight the hexadecimal color number (underneath the Blue value) and press Command-C (PC: Control-C) to Copy it.

Next, double-click on the last (far right) white color stop and in the Color Picker, press Command-V (PC: Control-V) to Paste the hexadecimal color number in its field (this is a simple way to ensure both color stops are the same color). Then click below the color bar, roughly in the middle, to add another color stop. Double-click on the new color stop and change the color to white in the Color Picker. As you do these operations, you'll see the effects you're having on the image.

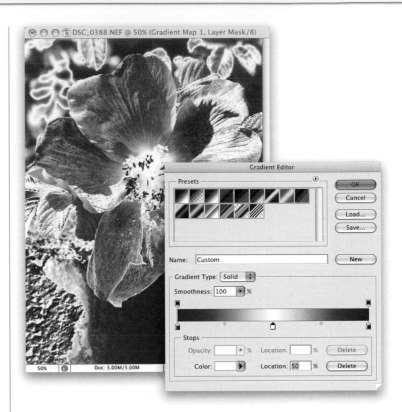

Step Four:

Continue to experiment with different colors for the color stops, and click-and-drag the color midpoints (the small diamond shapes between the color stops) to vary the distance of the blend between colors.

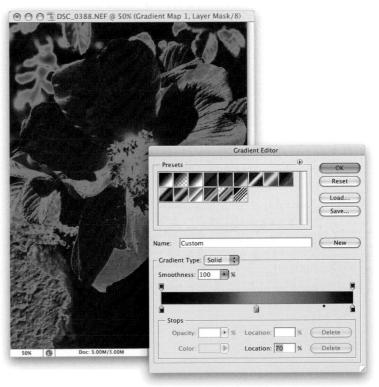

Variation 1: Radial gradient

variations:

Here I used the Gradient tool (G) to paint with a Radial gradient in black on the layer mask so the original flower shows through in the center.

In this case, I Control-clicked (PC: Right-clicked) on the adjustment layer and chose Blending Options. Then I held down the Option key (PC: Alt key) and split the black and white This Layer Blend If sliders, dragging until I liked the results. (For more on this, see Blending Options in the Key Concepts.)

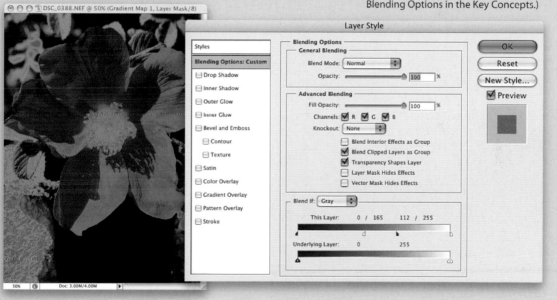

Variation 2: Split Blend If sliders

TECHNIQUE #46

This example has the Blending Options as in the previous variation, and a Radial gradient as in the first variation.

Variation 3: Combined Variations 1 and 2

Here I copied the contents of the Red channel and then pressed-and-held the Option key (PC: Alt key) while I clicked on the layer mask. This allowed me to view the layer mask so that I could paste the copied channel and create a "photographic" mask.

Variation 4: Red channel as layer mask

key concepts:

adjustment
layers

split toning

This technique simulates the effect of split toning: combining warm and cool tones in the same image.

My original photo looks like this.

Step One:

Press Command-Option-~ (the Tilde key, right above the Tab key) (PC: Control-Alt-~) to load the highlights in the photograph.

> **NOTE**
> If the highlights keyboard shortcut doesn't work in Mac OS X Tiger, you'll have to go to System Preferences>Keyboard & Mouse and turn off the shortcut for Move Focus to Window Drawer.

Step Two:

Click on the Create New Adjustment Layer icon at the bottom of the Layers palette to add a Color Balance adjustment layer and in the resulting dialog, click on the Highlights radio button. Move the color sliders to change the color of the highlight areas.

Color Balance

Color Balance

Color Levels: -3 +23 -71

Cyan ———————————————— Red
Magenta ———————————————— Green
Yellow ———————————————— Blue

OK
Reset
☑ Preview

Tone Balance
○ Shadows   ○ Midtones   ● Highlights
☑ Preserve Luminosity

Step Three:

Click on the Midtones radio button and move the color sliders to alter the color of the midtones of the photo, using similar colors to the highlights. Click OK when you are done.

Color Balance

Color Balance

Color Levels: 0 0 -59

Cyan ———————————————— Red
Magenta ———————————————— Green
Yellow ———————————————— Blue

OK
Reset
☑ Preview

Tone Balance
○ Shadows   ● Midtones   ○ Highlights
☑ Preserve Luminosity

mexicobeach.psd @ 50% (Color Balance 4, RGB/8)

50%   Doc: 4.30M/8.61M

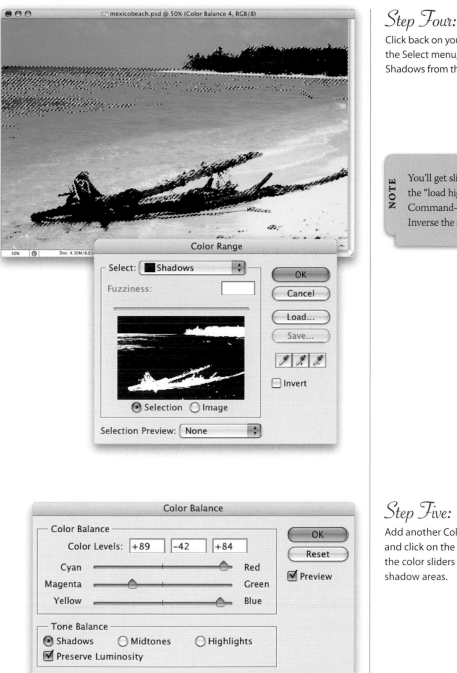

Step Four:

Click back on your Background layer, and from the Select menu, choose Color Range and pick Shadows from the Select pop-up menu.

NOTE You'll get slightly different results if you use the "load highlights" shortcut and press Command-Shift-I (PC: Control-Shift-I) to Inverse the selection.

Step Five:

Add another Color Balance adjustment layer and click on the Shadows radio button. Move the color sliders to change the color of the shadow areas.

271

Click on the Midtones radio button and move the color sliders to alter the color of the midtones of the photo, using similar colors to the shadows.

Here's the finished product.

Variation 1: Channel Mixer adjustment layer added

variations:

In this example, I added a Channel Mixer adjustment layer (below the other two adjustment layers) to make the image monochrome and make the warm and cool toning more apparent.

Instead of starting with a selection of the highlights and shadows, this version uses two Hue/Saturation adjustment layers and Blending Options.

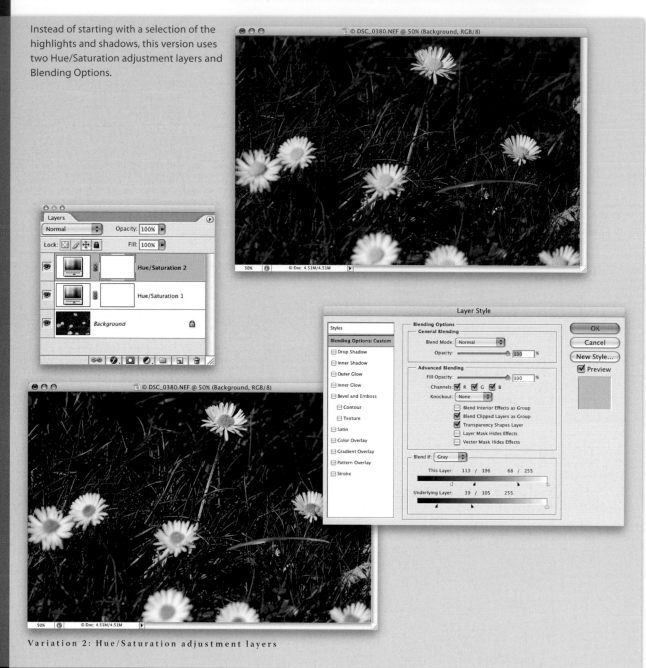

Variation 2: Hue/Saturation adjustment layers

Adobe Lightroom has its own built-in option called Split Toning, as shown here.

Variation 3: Split Toning in Adobe Lightroom

infrared simulation

This technique attempts to simulate infrared photography, where green foliage looks white and blue skies look close to black. This one will take a little bit of experimenting on your part, but with a bit of effort you can get some interesting results.

key concepts:

adjustment layers

blending options

Here's the original photo.

Step One:

Depending on your photo, you may want to add more overall saturation to the photo, and specifically more saturation to the greens. Here I clicked on the Create New Adjustment Layer icon at the bottom of the Layers palette and added a Hue/Saturation adjustment layer.

Hue/Saturation

Edit: Master

Hue: 0

Saturation: +16

Lightness: 0

OK
Reset
Load...
Save...

☐ Colorize
☑ Preview

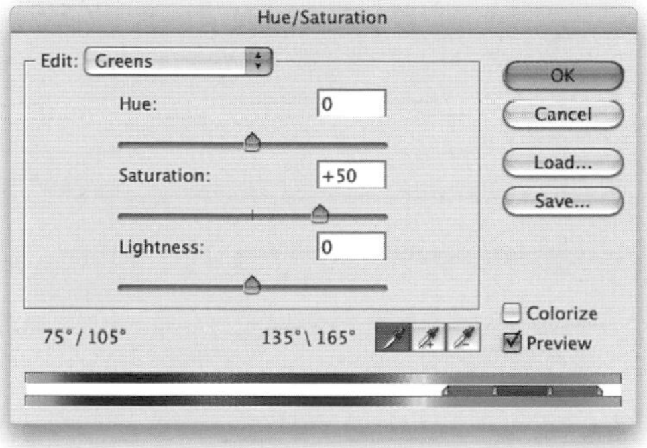

Hue/Saturation

Edit: Greens

Hue: 0

Saturation: +50

Lightness: 0

OK
Cancel
Load...
Save...

75° / 105°   135° \ 165°

☐ Colorize
☑ Preview

In the Hue/Saturation dialog, I added some saturation to the Master (all colors), and then chose Greens from the Edit pop-up menu and pumped up the saturation slider for it, too.

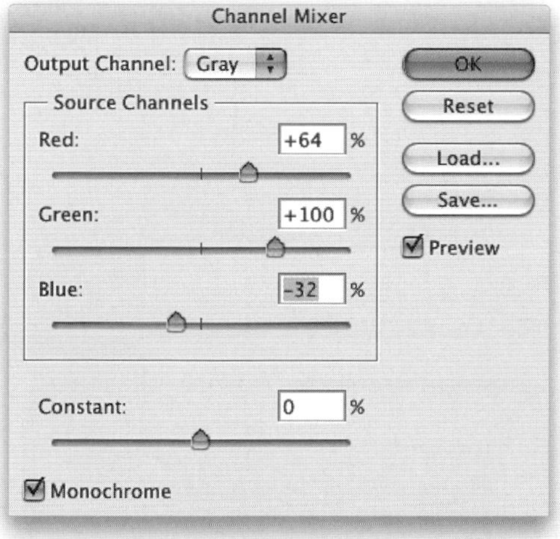

Channel Mixer

Output Channel: Gray

Source Channels

Red: +64 %

Green: +100 %

Blue: -32 %

Constant: 0 %

☑ Monochrome

OK
Reset
Load...
Save...
☑ Preview

Step Two:

Next, click back on your Background layer and add a Channel Mixer adjustment layer. Turn on the Monochrome checkbox and move the Source Channels sliders, using the rough guideline of having the three amounts add up to approximately 200.

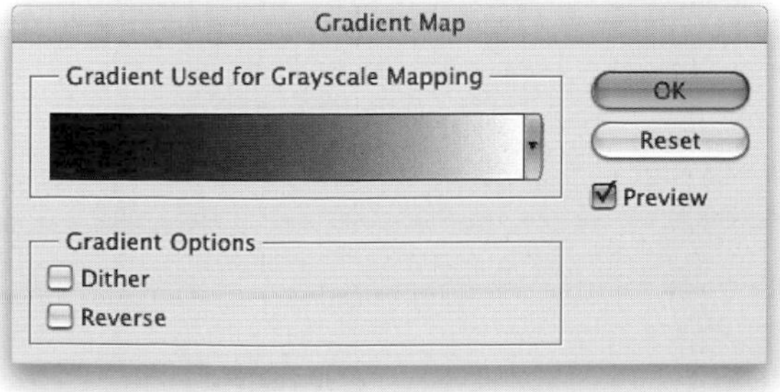

Gradient Map

Gradient Used for Grayscale Mapping

Gradient Options
☐ Dither
☐ Reverse

OK
Reset
☑ Preview

Step Three:

Click on your Background layer again, and press D to make sure your Foreground and Background colors are the default black and white. Then add a Gradient Map adjustment layer. Click on the gradient thumbnail in the Gradient Map dialog to open the Gradient Editor. Make sure the top-left gradient (Foreground to Background) is selected.

Step Four:

Press-and-hold the Option key (PC: Alt key) while you click-and-drag the right-hand (white) color stop to copy it and create another white color stop.

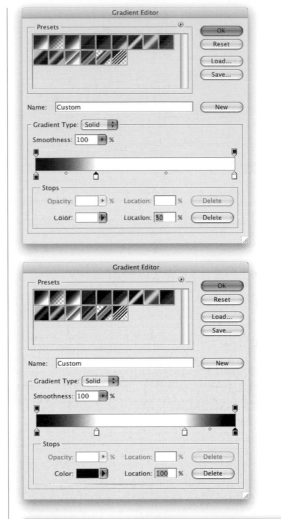

Use the same method to create another white color stop, and then double-click on the far right color stop to bring up the Color Picker. Change the color stop to black, as shown here.

As you make these changes to the gradient, you can see the effects on your photo.

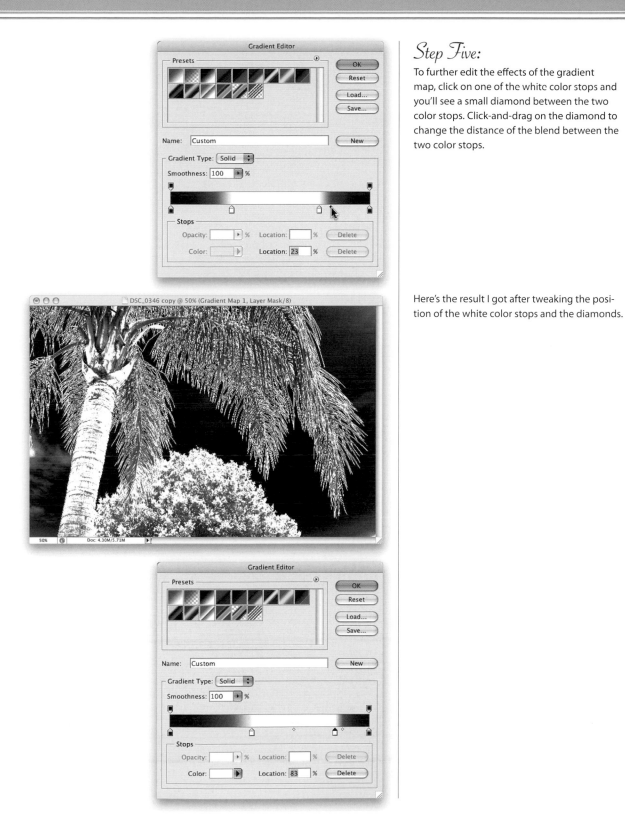

Step Five:

To further edit the effects of the gradient map, click on one of the white color stops and you'll see a small diamond between the two color stops. Click-and-drag on the diamond to change the distance of the blend between the two color stops.

Here's the result I got after tweaking the position of the white color stops and the diamonds.

Step Six:

Control-click (PC: Right-click) on the Gradient Map adjustment layer and choose Blending Options. Press-and-hold the Option key (PC: Alt key) and click on the black Underlying Layer Blend If slider. Drag the right side of the black slider to the right, approximately halfway, until some of the black starts to show through.

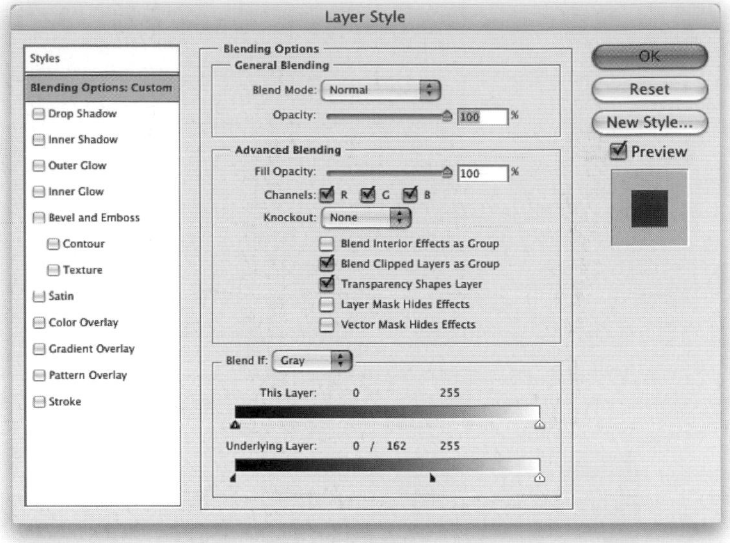

Here's another example with the same technique applied.

variation:

Here I clicked on the original Background layer and, from the Select menu, chose Color Range, where I selected Highlights. I added a new layer on top of the layer stack, filled the selection with white, and changed the layer blend mode to Soft Light.

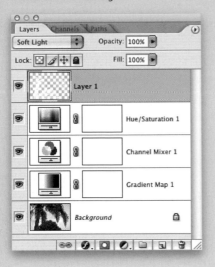

Variation 1: Highlights filled with white, set to Soft Light

key concepts:

filters

quick mask

layer masks

selective blurring

Here, we'll work with multiple layers and layer masks to selectively blur— and sharpen—different parts of an image.

Here's my original image.

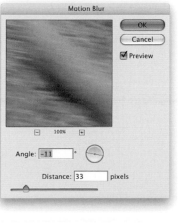

Step One:

Press Command-J (PC: Control-J) to duplicate the Background layer. To this copied Background layer, apply some form of blurring (under Filter>Blur). In this case, I used Motion Blur, since my photo had some motion in it. Lower the opacity of this layer to lessen the effect slightly.

Step Two:

Make a selection of the area that you want to be blurry. Here I used the Lasso tool (L) to make a basic selection of the water.

Step Three:

Since I only wanted the main edge of my selection to have feathering, I didn't apply feathering to the entire selection. Instead, I pressed Q to switch to Quick Mask mode and made a rough selection around the edge of the mask. Then I applied a Gaussian Blur (Filter>Blur>Gaussian Blur) to the mask, in effect applying feathering to just that edge. Press Q again to return to Standard mode.

Step Four:

Click on the Add Layer Mask icon at the bottom of the Layers palette to mask the area you don't want to be blurry (i.e., to hide the blurry layer in that area).

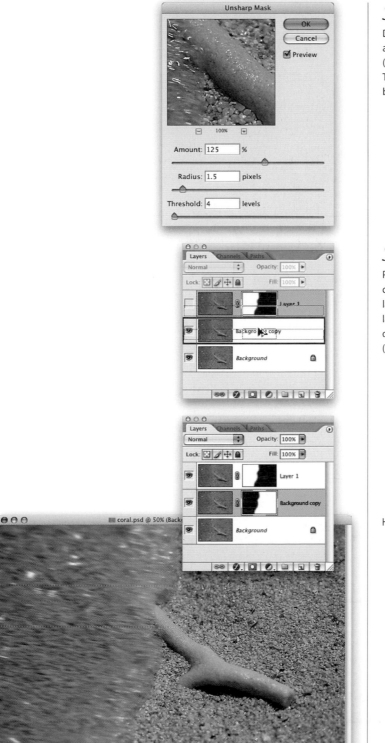

Step Five:

Duplicate the Background layer again and apply the Unsharp Mask filter (Filter>Sharpen>Unsharp Mask) to the copy. These are the settings I used—yours may well be different, depending on your photo.

Step Six:

Press-and-hold the Option key (PC: Alt key) and click-and-drag the layer mask from the blurry layer to this sharpened layer. That will copy the layer mask, but we need the mask to affect the opposite part of the photo, so press Command-I (PC: Control-I) to Invert the mask.

Here's the result.

variation:

In this example, I didn't have a specific area I wanted to be blurry, so after duplicating and blurring the photo, I added a layer mask and used the Gradient tool (G) on the mask to gradually fade the blurry area. Then I selected several areas that I wanted to be slightly blurry and filled them with either a gradient or 50% gray.

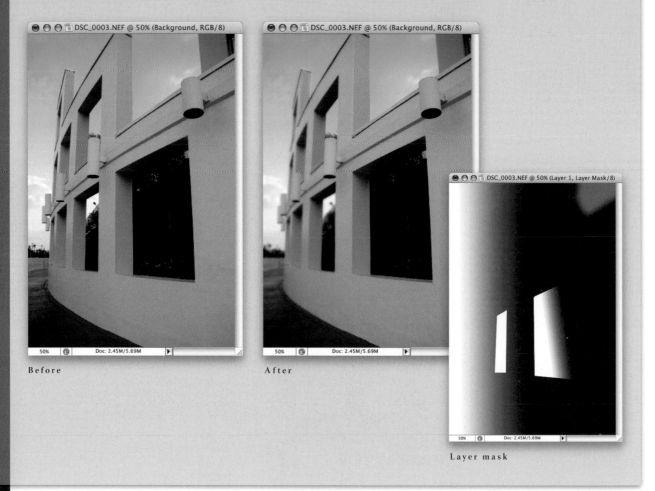

Before

After

Layer mask

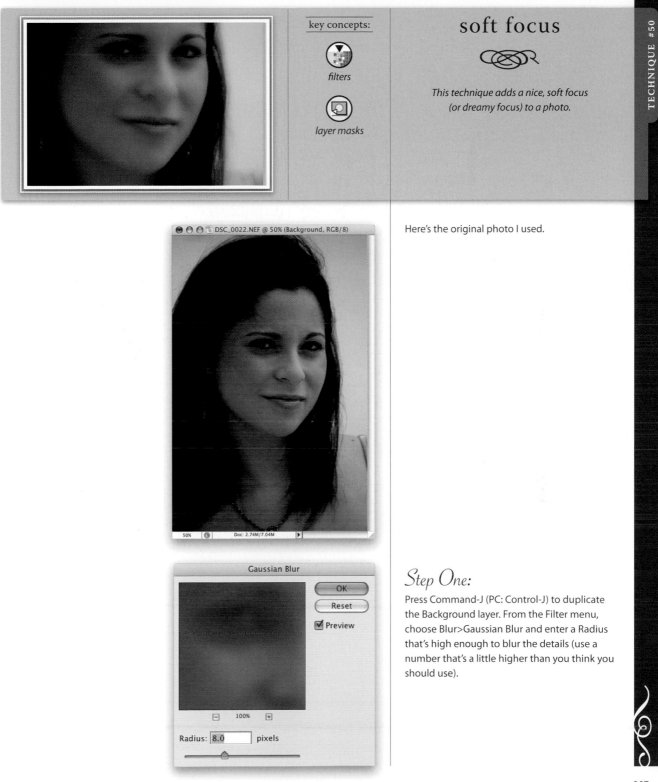

key concepts:

filters

layer masks

soft focus

This technique adds a nice, soft focus (or dreamy focus) to a photo.

Here's the original photo I used.

Step One:

Press Command-J (PC: Control-J) to duplicate the Background layer. From the Filter menu, choose Blur>Gaussian Blur and enter a Radius that's high enough to blur the details (use a number that's a little higher than you think you should use).

DSC_0022.NEF @ 50% (Background, RGB/8)

50%   Doc: 2.74M/7.04M

Gaussian Blur

OK

Reset

☑ Preview

100%

Radius: 8.0 pixels

Step Two:

Lower the opacity of the blurry layer—even changing the opacity to 90% will have an effect. Of course, it will vary with the photo, but somewhere in the 50–65% range is pretty typical.

Step Three:

You could stop at Step Two, but if there are details in the photo that look a little too blurry, you can add a layer mask and hide some areas of the blurry layer. Here I clicked on the Add Layer Mask icon at the bottom of the Layers palette to add a mask to the blurry layer, and pressed D, then X to set my Foreground to black. Then, I got the Brush tool (B) and painted with black over her eyes, lips, and hair. You could also paint with gray to slightly lower the opacity of the blurry layer.

Step Four:

As an optional step, click on the Background layer and then press Command-Option-~ (the Tilde key, right above your Tab key) (PC: Control-Alt-~) to load the highlights in the photograph. Then Press Command-J (PC: Control-J) to duplicate the selected pixels.

If the highlights keyboard shortcut doesn't work in Mac OS X Tiger, you'll have to go to System Preferences>Keyboard & Mouse and turn off the shortcut for Move Focus to Window Drawer.

NOTE

288

Here are the results with the highlight pixel layer first below the blurry layer, and then above the blurry layer.

Highlights below the blurry layer

Highlights above the blurry layer

variations:

In this example, I used the Surface Blur filter rather than Gaussian Blur, lowered the layer opacity, and painted on the layer mask.

Variation 1: Surface Blur filter

Before

After

Okay, so this isn't really a variation, but I wanted to show you that this technique works on more than just portraits. On this photo I used the Surface Blur filter, lowered the opacity of the blurry layer, and painted with gray on the layer mask over the areas of the flower that I wanted to be sharper.

slide mounts

Do this once and you'll have a graphic you can use over and over again— and you'll save the original in such a way that you can edit it if necessary.

key concepts:

free transform

layer styles

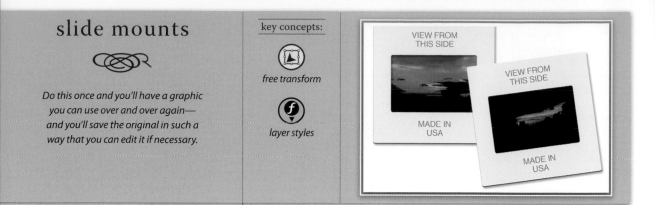

Step One:

Create a new document (press Command-N [PC: Control-N]) that is both physically larger and a higher resolution than you think you'll need. (Better to end up with a graphic that's too big that you can scale down, rather than one that's too small.) In my example, the document is 3x3" at a resolution of 300 ppi.

Step Two:

Add a blank layer to the document. Then, click on the Foreground color swatch at the bottom of the Toolbox to bring up the Color Picker. Pick an off-white color for the slide (I've started off with a darker color so it's easier to see here).

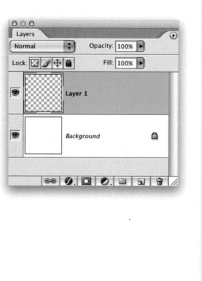

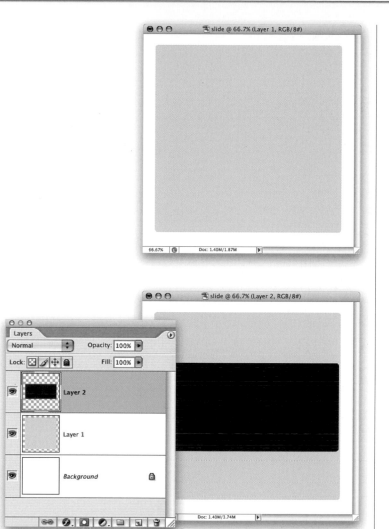

Step Three:

Click on the Rounded Rectangle tool (or press Shift-U until it comes up), and in the Options Bar, change the Radius to 10 pixels and click on the Fill Pixels icon (the third icon from the left). Press-and-hold the Shift key and click-and-drag to create the slide shape.

Step Four:

Add another new layer. Press D to change the Foreground color to black, and set the Radius to 3 pixels. Click-and-drag to create a shape that's the width of the slide shape and vertically centered, as shown here.

Step Five:

Press Command-T (PC: Control-T) for Free Transform. Press-and-hold the Option key (PC: Alt key), click on one of the side handles, and drag towards the center (the modifier key transforms towards the center). Press Return (PC: Enter) once you're done.

Step Six:

Command-click (PC: Control-click) on the thumbnail of the top layer to make a selection. Then, hide the top layer by clicking the Eye icon to the left of the thumbnail, click on the slide layer, and press Delete (PC: Backspace) to make a hole in your slide layer. Press Command-D (PC: Control-D) to Deselect.

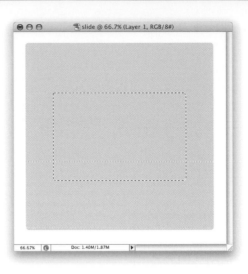

Step Seven:

With the slide layer active, click on the Add a Layer Style icon at the bottom of the Layers palette, and add a Bevel and Emboss layer style from the pop-up menu. In the Layer Style dialog, change the Size to 3 pixels.

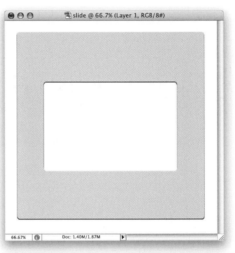

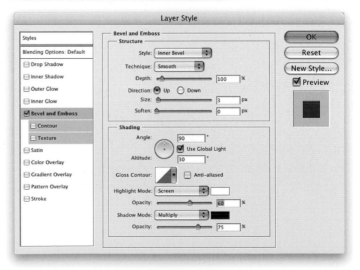

Step Eight:

With the Type tool (T), and the Caps Lock key on, click in the center of the slide's upper section. Click on the Center Text icon in the Options Bar, type "VIEW FROM," press Return (PC: Enter), and type "THIS SIDE." Use a simple typeface like Arial or Helvetica. Lower the opacity of the Type layer to around 35%.

Step Nine:

To make sure the text and the slide are perfectly aligned, Command-click (PC: Control-click) on the name of both layers in the Layers palette. Press V to get the Move tool and, in the Options Bar, click on the Align Horizontal Centers icon.

Step Ten:

Select just the Type layer and, holding down both Option and Shift (PC: Alt and Shift), click-and-drag the text down to the bottom of the slide. This will duplicate the Type layer, which you can then change to say "MADE IN (hard return) USA." Switch back to the Type tool and triple-click on the first line of copied text to highlight and type over it, then do the same for the second line of text. I also chose a lighter color for my slide (by changing the Foreground color), clicked on the slide layer, and then pressed Option-Shift-Delete (PC: Alt-Shift-Backspace) to fill only the existing pixels with the new color.

Step Eleven:

Hide the Background layer, click on the top layer, and then press Command-Option-Shift-E (PC: Control-Alt-Shift-E). This creates a merged copy of all the visible layers, while preserving all the original layers below. If you save this document as is, you'll have a flattened layer you can click-and-drag into other documents, and you'll have the original layers in case you want to change anything.

Here's how you can use the slide mount: Using the Move tool, click-and-drag the merged layer into another document. If it's too large, use Free Transform (with the Shift key held down) to scale down the size of the slide. Then you drag in a photo, position it below the slide layer and use Free Transform to scale the photo to fit in the slide.

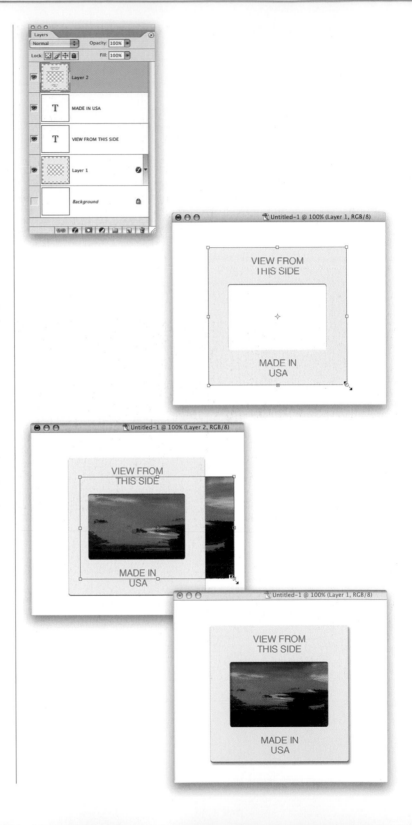

Variation 1

variations:

In this example, I duplicated the slide layer, dropped in a second photo, and then used Free Transform to rotate both the slide and its photo.

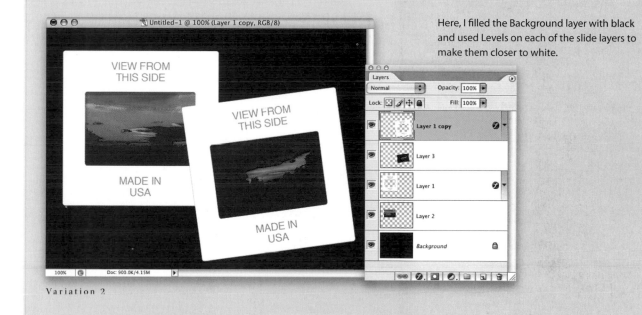

Variation 2

Here, I filled the Background layer with black and used Levels on each of the slide layers to make them closer to white.

creating a filmstrip

Create this filmstrip once using Shape layers and you'll have a template you can reuse— and that can easily be scaled to different sizes.

key concepts:

free transform

adjustment layers

Step One:

Create a new document that's larger than you need. My document was 7x5" at a resolution of 200 ppi (using Shape layers means that you can resize the filmstrip later if you need to). Press D to set black as the Foreground color, and click on the Rectangle tool (U). In the Options Bar, click on the first icon (Shape Layers), and click-and-drag on your document to create a rectangle. Press Return (PC: Enter) to accept your rectangle.

Step Two:

Press Shift-U to change to the Rounded Rectangle tool, and in the Options Bar, change the Radius to 3 pixels. Click-and-drag a small rectangle and then press Command-Delete (PC: Control-Backspace) to fill it with white (as shown here).

Step Three:

With the Path Selection tool (A), click on the small rectangle. Press Command-Option-T (PC: Control-Alt-T) to open Free Transform (with an enhanced function, as you'll see). Press-and-hold the Option and Shift keys (PC: Alt and Shift keys), click inside the rectangle (avoid the center reference point) and drag to the right. Pressing Option and Shift when you drag allows your copy of the small rectangle to move in only one direction, so you can keep them on a straight line horizontally. Press Return (PC: Enter). *Hint:* You may need to zoom in to avoid moving the center reference point.

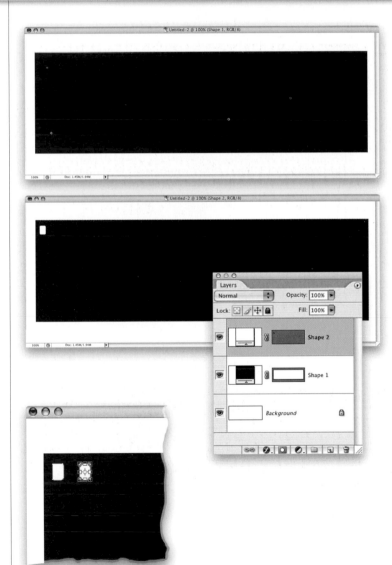

Step Four:

Press Command-Option-Shift-T (PC: Control-Alt-Shift-T) to Free Transform again, and it automatically makes another rectangle the same distance apart. Repeat the same shortcut multiple times to create a row of rectangles across the top of your filmstrip.

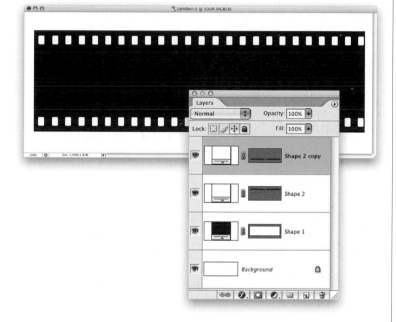

Step Five:

Press Command-J (PC: Control-J) to duplicate the Shape layer. Use the Move tool (V) with the Shift key held down to click-and-drag the shapes down to the bottom of your image.

Step Six:

Choose the Rectangle tool again, and click-and-drag a rectangle that's a little less than a third of the width of the black rectangle. In my example, the rectangle is approximately the width of eight of the small, white rectangles.

Step Seven:

Use the Path Selection tool to click on the white rectangle you just created. Press Command-Option-T, hold down Option and Shift, and click-and-drag the rectangle to the right, leaving a small border between the rectangles. Press Command-Option-Shift-T to make a third copy with the same border.

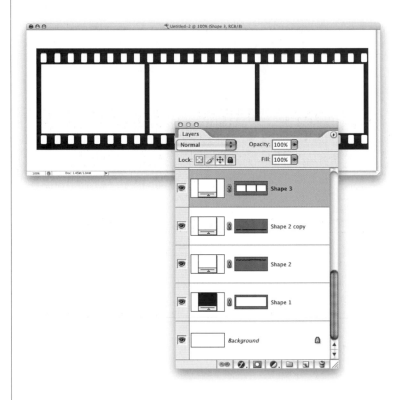

Step Eight:

Ideally, the small rectangles will line up with the three large rectangles. In my case, they didn't, but it is easy to fix. With the Path Selection tool, click on the last rectangle, press-and-hold the Shift key and click-and-drag the rectangle to the left so it lines up with the edge of the large rectangle.

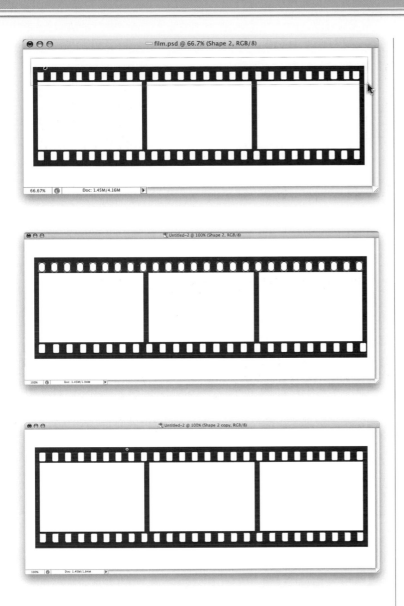

Step Nine:

Using the Path Selection tool, click-and-drag a selection around all the small rectangles. In the Options Bar, click on the Distribute Horizontal Centers icon (the second icon from the right). Repeat these last two steps for the bottom set of rectangles.

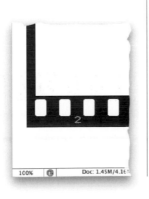

Step Ten:

Use the Type tool (T) to add numbers to the filmstrip. I used Arial Rounded as the typeface with a small size, chose a gold color, and positioned the first number between the second and third rectangles.

With the Move tool selected, press-and-hold the Option key (PC: Alt key) and click-and-drag the Type layer approximately four rectangles to the right to copy it, adding an "A" after the number. Copy the Type layer enough times to number across the bottom of the filmstrip.

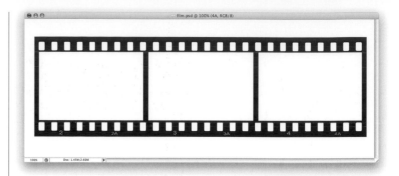

Step Eleven:

Hide the Background layer by clicking on the Eye icon to the left of the layer thumbnail, and then press Command-Option-Shift-E (PC: Control-Alt-Shift-E) to merge the visible layers into a flattened copy layer. Click-and-drag this layer to the top of the layer stack.

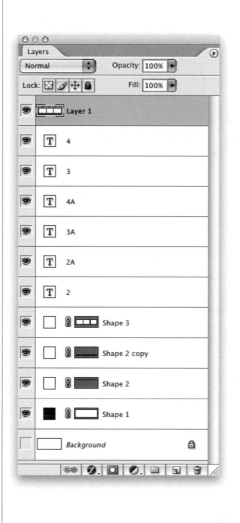

Step Twelve:

Hide your Shape layers, and with your new merged layer active, Command-click (PC: Control-click) on the thumbnail of one of the small rectangle layers to load a selection of the layer. Then press Delete (PC: Backspace) and Command-D (PC: Control-D) to Deselect. Repeat for the other small rectangle layer.

Save the document as is, with the merged layer on top and the original layers below—that way you can edit the original layers should you wish to make any changes, and you have a finished filmstrip layer ready to drag into a document.

Step Thirteen:

To use the filmstrip in another document, use the Move tool to drag the top merged layer into your document. If necessary, use Free Transform (Command-T [PC: Control-T]) to scale and/or rotate the filmstrip.

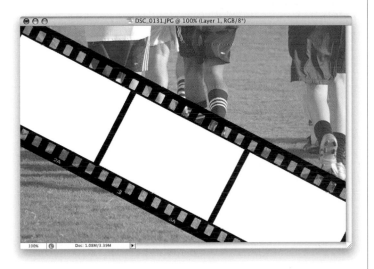

Then, use the Magic Wand tool (W) to select one of the white rectangles.

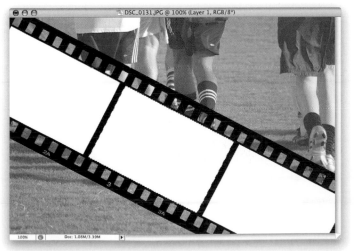

Open the photo you want to use, press Command-A (PC: Control-A) to Select All, and press Command-C (PC: Control-C) to Copy the photo. Then, switch back to the image with the filmstrip, and use Edit>Paste Into. Use Free Transform to rotate and scale the photo.

Here's my finished version with three photos pasted into the filmstrip and a Levels adjustment layer to lighten the background photo.

key concepts:

free transform

one photo, two sizes

This simple technique uses the same photo twice—next year's Christmas card, possibly?

Here's the original photo I used in my example.

Step One:

Press Command-J (PC: Control-J) to duplicate the Background layer. Press Command-T (PC: Control-T) for Free Transform, and then hold down Option and Shift (PC: Alt and Shift) while you click-and-drag a corner handle to scale the copy down to the size you want. Don't commit your transformation yet, though.

305

Step Two:

After positioning the copy layer where you want it, press Return (PC: Enter) to commit the transformation. Command-click (PC: Control-click) on the layer thumbnail to load it as a selection.

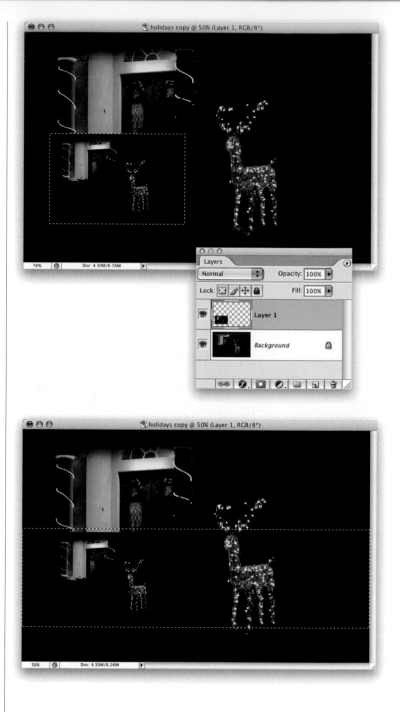

Step Three:

From the Select menu, choose Transform Selection. Press-and-hold the Option key (PC: Alt key), click on one of the side handles and drag the selection to make it the width of your photo. If you want, use the same method to make the height of the selection slightly bigger than the small photo. When it is the size you want, press Return (PC: Enter) to set the selection.

Step Four:

Command-click on the Create a New Layer icon at the bottom of the Layers palette to add a new layer below the copied Background layer. Press D to set your Foreground and Background colors to the default, and press Command-Delete (PC: Control-Backspace) to fill the selection with white. Lower the Opacity of the white layer to around 30–40%. Press Command-D (PC: Control-D) to Deselect.

Step Five:

Click on the Foreground color swatch at the bottom of the Toolbox and choose a color that will complement your photo. With the Type tool (T), click to the right of your small image to add a Type layer with whatever wording and style is appropriate for your photo.

variations:

Here I applied a slight Gaussian Blur
(Filter>Blur>Gaussian Blur) to the white layer
to soften the edges, and a Drop Shadow layer
style to the text.

Variation 1

In this case, I duplicated the Background
layer, applied a Gaussian Blur, and lowered
the opacity to create a soft focus effect on the
background photo.

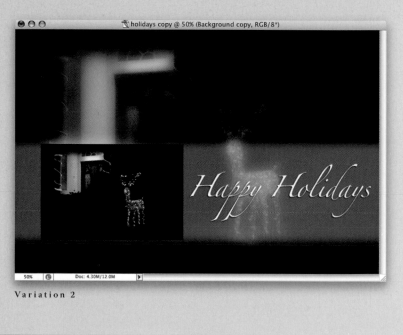

Variation 2

Here's a different photo that uses a vertical format and blue as the color of the rectangle.

Variation 3

photo grid

If you have a collection of similar photos that you want to put together, you can do this pretty easily using the Auto Select Layer and Align features. I used nine photos in my example.

key concepts:

free transform

Step One:

With the Shift key held down, click-and-drag with the Rectangular Marquee tool (M) to create a square selection in your image.

Step Two:

Press Command-N (PC: Control-N) to create a new document, and use the Move tool (V) to drag-and-drop the selected pixels into the new document. Press Command-T (PC: Control-T) for Free Transform, and then scale the size down (with the Shift key held down to constrain the proportions).

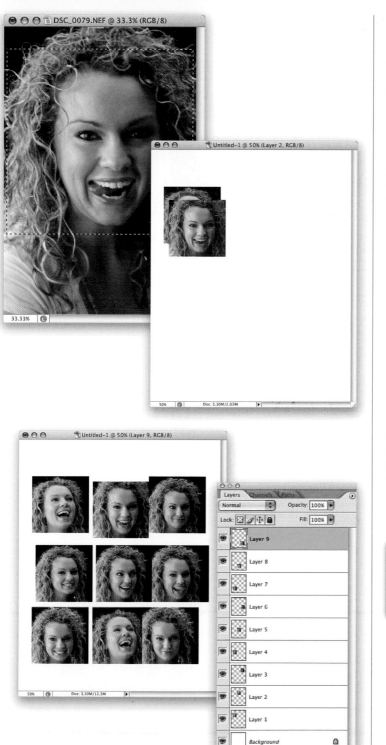

Step Three:

Switch back to the Rectangular Marquee tool, and drag-and-drop the selection border (the marching ants) from the first photo onto the second photo. Use the Move tool to drag-and-drop the selected pixels into the new document.

Step Four:

Press Command-Shift-T (PC: Control-Shift-T) to apply the same transformation to the second image.

Repeat Steps Three and Four until you have a square selection of all your photos copied onto the main document. Don't worry if the images are not aligned—we'll do that next.

HINT

Use keyboard shortcuts to switch back and forth between the Rectangular Marquee and Move tools: M for Rectangular Marquee and V for Move.

Step Five:

With the Move tool selected, turn on the Auto Select Layer checkbox in the Options Bar. Click-and-drag across the top three photos to select those layers.

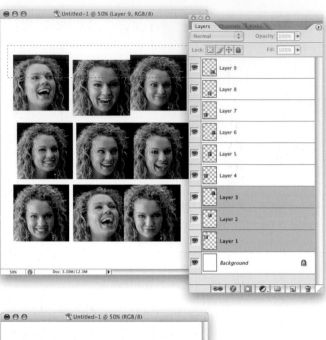

Then, in the Options Bar, click on the Align Top Edges icon (the first alignment icon on the left).

Step Six:

If necessary, click on the top-left photo and nudge it to the left, then click on the top-right photo and nudge it to the right. Click-and-drag to select all three of the top photos and then click on the Distribute Horizontal Centers icon (the second alignment icon from the right).

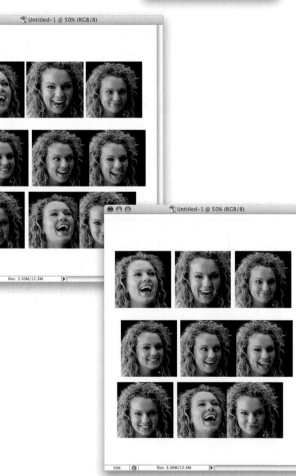

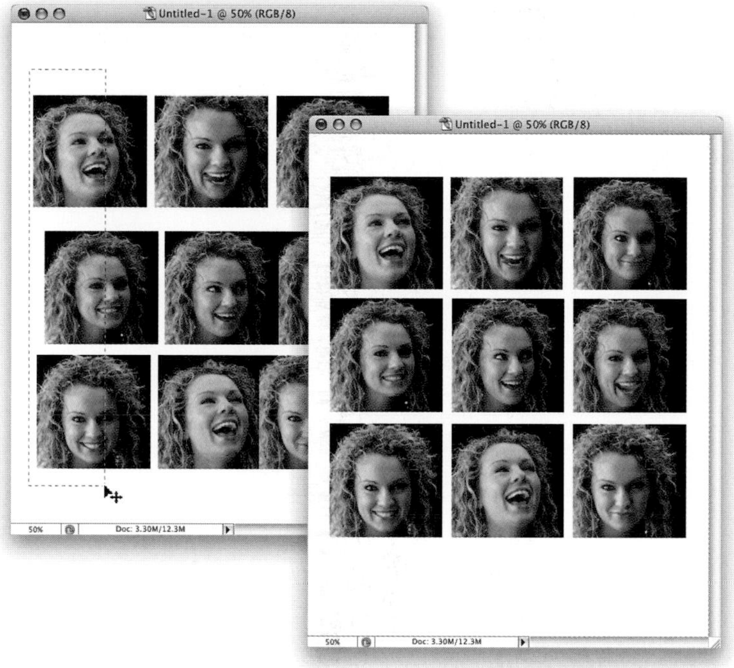

Step Seven:

Click-and-drag to select the three photos on the left-hand side, and in the Options Bar, click on the Align Left Edges icon (the fourth alignment icon from the left).

Continue selecting and aligning/distributing layers until you have an even grid of photos. Click-and-drag around all of the photos to select all the layers, and then click-and-drag the grid of photos to the center of the page.

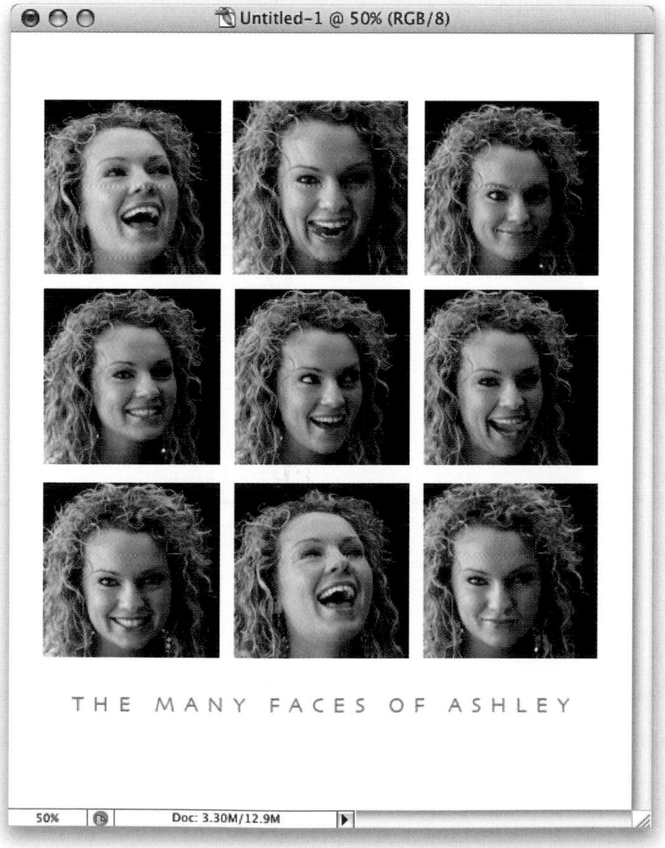

Here I added some text.

THE MANY FACES OF ASHLEY

variations:

In this example, I added a Hue/Saturation adjustment layer at the top of the layer stack and turned on the Colorize checkbox.

In Variation 2, I used four photos and added a thin stroke border around all four images.

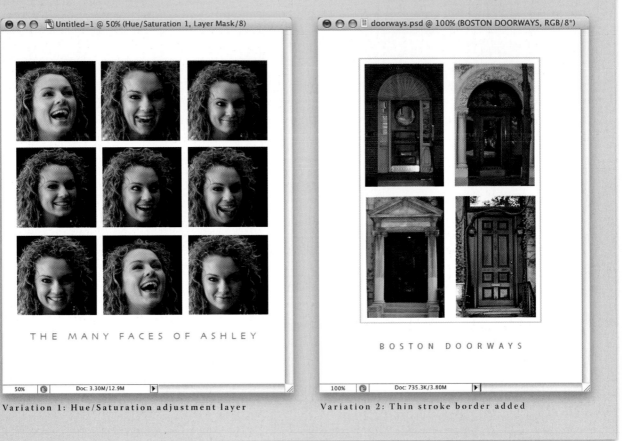

Variation 1: Hue/Saturation adjustment layer

Variation 2: Thin stroke border added

This variation uses a wide layout with a black background and four photos, each of which has a thin stroke border.

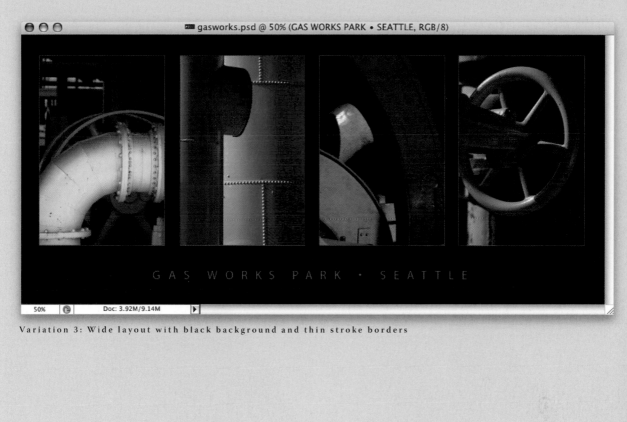

Variation 3: Wide layout with black background and thin stroke borders

IV

presenting your work

Nobody likes show-offs, but most of us do have a desire to show off our work, to say "take a look at this." This section is all about simple, yet effective, ways to help your work be seen, from simple Photoshop slide shows to customized websites. Think of it as the digital equivalent of the good old days when your parents stuck your artwork on the fridge using the magnet from your trip to California. (Come to think of it, my family's fridge magnets were pretty boring: real estate agents and plumbers, I believe. But that's neither here nor there, is it?)

So go ahead, show off your work! You deserve it after all your hard work cooking up a masterpiece. (See how we managed to come full circle there and return to the whole food thing? I feel much better now.)

photoshop slide shows

We'll look at three different ways to create a slide show in Photoshop (one in Adobe Bridge actually), each with its own advantages.

Full-Screen Slide Show

This method works best for one-off situations—when you want to show several images and are unlikely to show those same images together again.

Step One:

Open the photos you want in your slide show—and only those photos.

Step Two:

Press-and-hold the Shift key and click on the third screen mode icon at the bottom of the Toolbox (shown here). This will change all the images into Full Screen mode.

Step Three:

Press Tab to hide all floating palettes, then Control-Tab (both platforms) to change between images. You may have to use the Zoom In shortcut to make each image larger—Command-+ (PC: Control-+).

To return to normal view, press Tab to show the palettes, and Shift-click on the Standard Screen mode icon (the far-left icon at the bottom of the Toolbox).

Layer Comp Slide Show

There are two advantages to this method: you can save the document to run the show again, and once you've created a keyboard shortcut you can use it over and over again.

Step One:

Combine all the images for your slide show into one document by clicking-and-dragging them in one at a time with the Move tool (V), while holding down the Shift key so that all the layers are pin-registered (they line up perfectly on top of each other).

Step Two:

In the Layer Comps palette (found nested in the Palette Well by default), click on the Create New Layer Comp icon and give the layer comp a name.

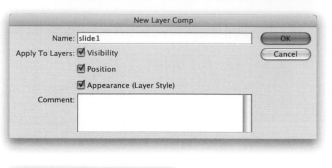

In the Layers palette, click on the Eye icon beside the top layer to hide it, then switch back to the Layer Comps palette and add a new layer comp for this view. Repeat this process until you have a layer comp that shows each layer.

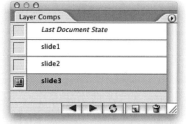

Step Three:

From the Edit menu, choose Keyboard Short-cuts, or press Command-Option-Shift-K (PC: Control-Alt-Shift-K). Choose Palette Menus from the Shortcuts For pop-up menu, scroll down to Layer Comps, and click on the right-facing triangle to see the commands. Click beside Next Layer Comp and enter the shortcut you'd like to use. Chances are, just about every shortcut you'll think of is taken, so you may have to override an existing shortcut as I've done here by choosing a shortcut used by the Actions palette for the Flip Horizontal action. If you choose a shortcut that is already taken, a warning will appear near the bottom of the dialog, as you can see here.

Now, create a shortcut for Previous Layer Comp, as well.

Step Four:

To run your slide show, press Tab to hide your palettes, and press F twice to change to Full Screen mode. If necessary, use Command–+ (PC: Control–+) to Zoom In, then press your shortcut for Next Layer Comp to run your slide show.

> **NOTE**
> If you used a shortcut that was used by the Actions palette, you may have to find that action, double-click on it to open the Action Options dialog, and remove the shortcut from the action by choosing None in the Function Key pop-up menu.

To return to a normal view, press Tab to show the palettes, and F to return to Standard Screen mode.

Bridge Slide Show

Since it's a built-in function of Bridge, this slide show is always available and it's easy to use—and you don't have to have the photos open to run the show.

Step One:

In Bridge, select the photos you want to show by Command-clicking (PC: Control-clicking) on them (if you want every image included, you can skip to the next step without selecting anything).

Step Two:

Press Command-L (PC: Control-L) to open the slide show, then the Spacebar to start it. You can also press H to access various slide show controls. Press Escape to end the show and return to Bridge.

> **NOTE**
> You can use the Bridge slide show to rank your image by pressing 1–5, or open an image by pressing O.

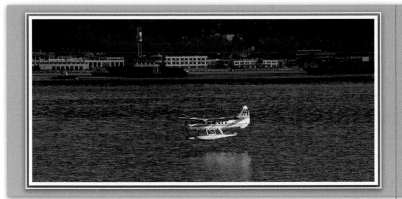

pdf presentation

This built-in function lets you create self-running slide shows that anyone can view with the Adobe Acrobat Reader. With one important step during its creation, you can ensure that your images are secure.

Step One:

In Bridge, select the photos you want to include in your PDF slide show. (Command-click [PC: Control-click] on each image to select multiple images.)

Step Two:

From the Tools menu, choose Photoshop>PDF Presentation. The first time you use this dialog you'll probably have to change the Output Options to Presentation. (Even though it's called PDF Presentation, the default choice is Multi-Page Document. Go figure.) In Presentation Options, set the delay between slides, turn on the Loop After Last Page checkbox if you want, and pick a transition effect.

If you decide at this point to change the order of the images in the presentation, you can click-and-drag to change the order of the files in the list. Needless to say, it would be more effective (and more visual) to set the order in Bridge before you run the command.

Step Three:

Click Save and name the PDF file. In the subsequent Save Adobe PDF dialog, you'll set the options for the PDF file. First, choose Smallest File Size from the Adobe PDF Preset pop-up menu (this assumes you want to email a small file—of course, you can create larger PDF files if you want).

TECHNIQUE #56

Step Four:

To create a PDF file of your images that can only be viewed (not saved in another format or printed), click on Security in the list on the left side of the dialog and, under Permissions, turn on the Use a Password to Restrict Printing, Editing and Other Tasks checkbox. Enter a Permissions Password and leave the other options as they are (Printing Allowed: None, Changes Allowed: None, and the two Enable checkboxes turned off).

After clicking Save PDF, you'll be asked to confirm the password you just created.

vancouver-show.pdf

A PDF file will be created that can be emailed and opened in Acrobat Reader or Acrobat Pro. When the file is opened, the slide show will automatically run, and after pressing Escape to end the show, the Print option will be grayed out.

NOTE One common complaint about Photoshop's PDF Presentation is that you cannot automatically add filenames to each image. Thanks to my buddy Matt Kloskowski, now you can with a script you can download from www.photoshopfinishingtouches.com.

smart picture package

key concepts:

free transform

Although Photoshop has a built-in function called Picture Package, it's pretty difficult to personalize it. You can create your own layouts, but it's next to impossible to add your logo or change the color of the page. Here's an alternative.

If you've ever tried to alter a picture package in Photoshop, you know how frustrating it can be. Then along comes my pal Matt Kloskowski and his *Photoshop CS2 Speed Clinic* book with this great idea: make the equivalent of a picture package using Smart Objects. I tweaked the idea just a bit by adding some personalization.

Step One:

Press Command-N (PC: Control-N) to create a new document in the size you want: I created an 8x10" page at the resolution needed for my inkjet printer. From the File menu, choose Place and navigate to the image you want to use. Once it appears on the page, use the handles to resize it.

By using the Place command, a Smart Object is created, giving you lots of sizing control.

NOTE

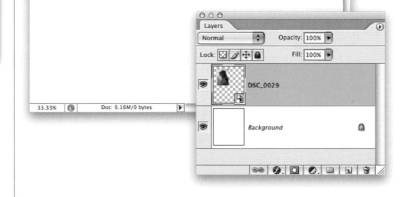

Step Two:

With the Move tool (V), hold down Option and Shift (PC: Alt and Shift) while you click-and-drag on the image to create a copy of the Smart Object layer. (You could also duplicate the layer and then move it into position.) Continue copying the Smart Object until you have the number of images you want (each on a separate layer). As you can see in this example, you can also use Free Transform (Command-T [PC: Control-T]) or the Edit>Transform menu commands to rotate and scale the Smart Objects.

Step Three:

Add your logo, name, contact information, etc. and save the document as a PSD template that you can use over and over again.

TECHNIQUE #57

327

Using this same layout with a different photo is simple, thanks to Smart Objects. Control-click (PC: Right-click) on any of the Smart Object layers and from the contextual menu, choose Replace Contents. Choose a different photo and all of the photos will change (while preserving the position and size of each image).

In this example, I replaced the original photo with an image in RAW format, which meant that first Camera Raw opened, and after I made my adjustments, the photos were replaced with the adjusted photo.

> **NOTE**
> If you double-click on a Smart Object layer, the original file is opened for you to edit. If the Smart Object is based on a RAW file, it will automatically open Camera Raw for you to make further changes.

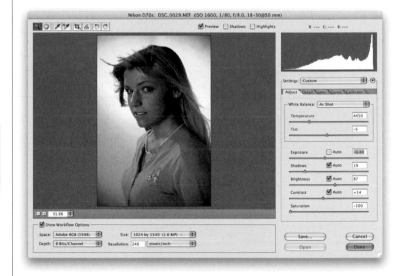

variations:

In Variation 1, I added some color to the Background layer and added a Stroke layer style to each Smart Object layer.

After using Replace Contents to pick a different photo, a new layout is created, again preserving the size, position, and layer style.

Variation 1: Added color to the Background layer   Variation 2: Replaced contents

web photo gallery

Here you'll see how to use the built-in automated website creation tool, Web Photo Gallery, and if you're a little more adventurous, how to customize the website.

Step One:

In Bridge, select the images you want to include on your website by Command-clicking (PC: Control-clicking) on them, and then from the Tools menu, select Photoshop>Web Photo Gallery.

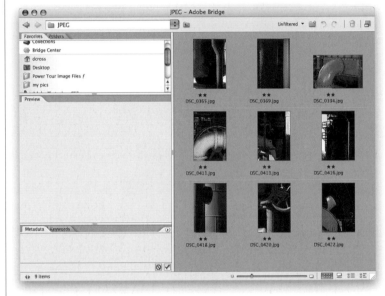

Step Two:

Choose the gallery style you'd like—you'll have to live with the fact that the preview is a little on the small side. You also want to indicate the destination for the results of the automated command—I recommend creating a separate folder.

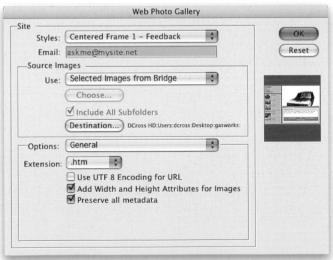

Step Three:

In the Options pop-up menu, choose Banner, and then enter the name of the site, the photographer's name, and the contact information. The date should default to the current date, but of course, you can always change it.

Step Four:

In the Options pop-up menu, choose Large Images, and then decide on the image size and quality, and the information you'd like to appear in your Web gallery.

Step Five:

In the Options pop-up menu, choose Thumbnails, and determine the size you'd like them to be and if you want the filename to appear.

Step Six:

In the Options pop-up menu, choose Custom Colors, and change colors if you like (you cannot change all the colors in the layout, just the ones indicated here).

Step Seven:

In the Options pop-up menu, choose Security (if you want to add copyright information). Enter the custom text you'd like to appear on the large images, and choose the font attributes, color, and opacity.

Step Eight:

Click OK to start the automated function. From there, Photoshop will take over, and after a few moments (depending on the number of images) you'll get a preview in your browser.

NOTE

At this point, you are viewing a working version of your website on your local hard drive. To turn this into a live site, you'll need a Web server and software to upload to the server the entire Web Photo Gallery folder.

333

Not for the Faint of Heart...

In order to customize a Web Photo Gallery template, you'll have to open the HTML pages and make the changes there. If you've never worked with any Web authoring tools, I'll get my warning out of the way right now and tell you to be careful! The best plan is to find and copy the folder that contains the Web style you want to customize.

You'll find the Web templates in Hard Drive: Applications:Photoshop CS2:Presets:Web Photo Gallery on a Mac or C:\Program Files\ Adobe\Adobe Photoshop CS2\Presets\Web Photo Gallery on a PC.

Duplicate the entire folder within the same Presets folder location so that your copy will appear in the Web Photo Gallery dialog.

To make changes to the template, you'll need to use a Web authoring tool, such as Dreamweaver or Adobe GoLive, or a text editor. Here I opened the file called FrameSet in GoLive (depending on the template, the main page may be named slightly differently). I added a small logo and saved the file—it's important that you keep the same name and save it in the same location.

Then I ran the Web Photo Gallery again, this time choosing my newly edited copy of the template.

You can also edit (again, with caution) something called tokens, which determine the size and position of information, such as the site name. (For more information on customizing the gallery and tokens, look in the Adobe Help Center, searching "web gallery.") Tokens always display with "%" at the beginning and end of the name, such as %PHOTOGRAPHER%.

Here I moved the %PHOTOGRAPHER% token above the %HEADER% token and made it larger.

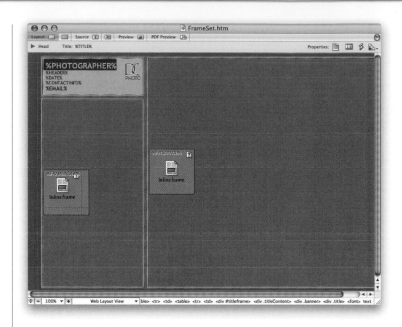

The result of running the Web Photo Gallery again is shown here.

In this case, I also changed the background color of the page in GoLive.

In case you didn't get the message about customizing Web Photo Gallery templates, let me say it again: Use extreme caution and make sure you're working on a *copy* of an existing template.

indesign contact sheet

Although Photoshop has a built-in automation called Contact Sheet II, it's pretty challenging to customize the results. Thankfully, Adobe InDesign also has a contact sheet and this one is pretty simple to customize—just about any way you want.

Step One:

In InDesign, create a new document that is the size you want for your contact sheet. Turn off the Facing Pages checkbox, choose the orientation of the page, and most importantly, set the margins. The area inside the margins determines where your photos will be placed, so if you want to add a logo to the bottom of the page, make that margin larger (as I've done here).

Step Two:

After the page has opened, in the Pages palette, double-click on the icon called A-Master to edit the master page. It's important that you put things like your logo on this master page so that it will appear on every page that is created.

Step Three:

Here I placed on the master page—outside the bottom margin—a Photoshop file that I had created and saved. You can make other changes in InDesign, such as adding a large colored rectangle (to change the page color).

Step Four:

Save the document as an InDesign template by choosing (oddly enough) InDesign CS2 Template from the Format pop-up menu in the Save As dialog.

Step Five:

Switch to Bridge and select the images you want in your contact sheet by Command-clicking (PC: Control-clicking) on them.

From the Tools menu, choose InDesign>Create InDesign Contact Sheet, and in the resulting dialog, set the options for your contact sheet: the layout (columns, rows, spacing, and rotation), any captions, whether you want to save it as a PDF, and most importantly, select the template you previously saved. Click OK.

Here's the result (shown in InDesign). It's important to note that every part of this layout remains fully editable, either by working on the master page to change master items, or by working with the elements on the page itself.

Optional:

A note about the captions created by the automated Create InDesign Contact Sheet command: the default font is Times 10 pt. Although you can easily change this after the layout has been created, it is also possible to change the font in your template. First, let's look at editing the font and size after you've run the automated command. In the Paragraph Styles palette, double-click on the style called "labels" to bring up the Paragraph Style Options dialog and pick a new font and size (under Basic Character Formats) or any other setting you'd like to change, such as alignment. All the labels in the document will update once you click OK.

To change the font in your template, in the Paragraph Styles palette, click on the Create New Style icon at the bottom of the palette to add a new style called "labels" (lower case). Then, double-click on it to bring up the Paragraph Style Options dialog and set the attributes in the Basic Character Formats.

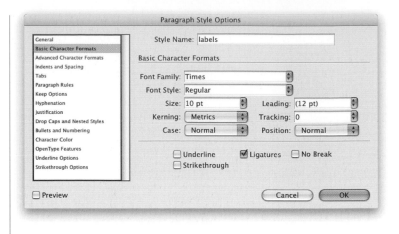

Although you can change the font, alignment, color, and other settings, it seems as though the label size will always default to 10 pt, regardless of the size you choose. Here I changed the font, alignment, color, and size for the label style in my template, but when I ran the Create InDesign Contact Sheet command, the size remained at 10 pt.

DSC_1541.JPG
Size: 1532 KB

variations:

I decided to use the InDesign contact sheet for a different purpose: to create a one-photo gallery layout. I created a template that was in landscape format with a black border and text at the bottom. Again, I made certain to set the margins for the positioning of the placed photograph. After saving the template, I selected one image in Bridge and used the Create InDesign Contact Sheet command, changing the rows and columns to 1 each (so that only one photo was imported). Here's the result.

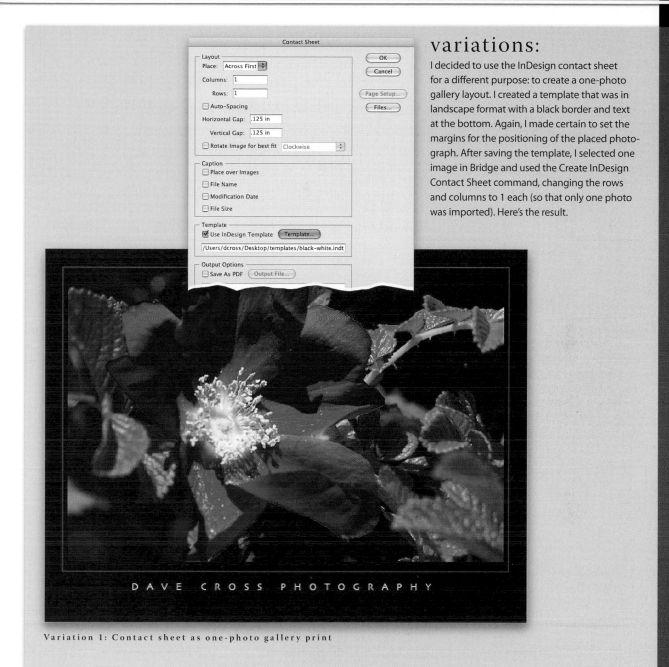

Variation 1: Contact sheet as one-photo gallery print

In this example, I placed a large lightened photo on the master page and altered the margins so that the contact sheet photos would only appear to the right of the model in the background photo.

DAVE CROSS
PHOTOGRAPHY

ODESSA, FL

Variation 2: Lightened photo as background

credits

All photos in this book are ©Dave Cross, except as indicated.

Some techniques in this book are based in part on ideas from the following: Matt Kloskowski, Scott Kelby, Eddie Tapp, Katrin Eismann, and Dan Margulis.

Sashi Luna, Miami, Florida

Sabrina Luna, Miami, Florida

Stevie Clark, Tampa, Florida

Ashley Simpson, Tampa, Florida

Madeline Madchen, Tampa, Florida

Ana Maria Reyes, Miami, Florida

Tom Bronson, Tampa, Florida

Index

Essential Plug-ins
for Digital Photographers

PhotoFrame 3 **NEW**

The all new PhotoFrame 3 is the essential border and edge effect plug-in that allows you to create unique border and edge effects. Complete with thousands of professionally designed frames that can be combined together to create an unlimited number of unique combinations, PhotoFrame lets you interactively design stunning border and edge effects in Photoshop™. PhotoFrame 3 includes thousands of new frames and is packed with new features including a built-in Frame Browser, Random Frame Generator and an all new Preview Window that allows you to compare multiple frames to each other at the same time.

"PhotoFrame is the only product I use to create edge effects that look as if I did them in the darkroom. When it comes to adding border and edge effects to my images, PhotoFrame is simply the best." — Jim DiVitale

Image © 2006 Jim DiVitale | Learn more about Jim at http://www.divitalephoto.com

Genuine Fractals™
Mask Pro™
 ─ **PhotoFrame**™
Intellihance Pro™

Photoshop plug-in suite

onOneSoftware.com

onOne software™

key concept quick card

Tear out the card as a quick reference for the Key Concepts used throughout the book. For more details, please refer to the Key Concepts section on page 1. The Key Concept Quick Card also includes some important shortcuts and additional Photoshop resources.

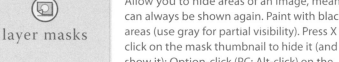

KEY CONCEPT

layer masks

p. 2

Allow you to hide areas of an image, meaning those pixels are never deleted, and can always be shown again. Paint with black to hide areas, paint with white to show areas (use gray for partial visibility). Press X to swap between black and white; Shift-click on the mask thumbnail to hide it (and show it); Option-click (PC: Alt-click) on the mask thumbnail to view the mask itself.

KEY CONCEPT

quick mask

p. 5

Use to view a selection as a colored overlay rather than selection edges. Paint with white to add to the selection, paint with black to deselect. You can also apply filters in Quick Mask mode. Press Q to toggle between Standard mode and Quick Mask mode.

KEY CONCEPT

define brush

p. 6

Start with a photo or paint a shape, make a selection, and then choose Edit> Define Brush Preset. Use the Brushes palette (in the Palette Well) to change settings such as Brush Tip Shape and Shape Dynamics or to apply a pattern as a texture in a brush.

KEY CONCEPT

define pattern

p. 8

Patterns can be incorporated into brush settings, used to fill a selection, or you can paint with a pattern using the Pattern Stamp tool. Creating a pattern is as simple as making a selection and choosing Edit>Define Pattern. Consider applying Threshold before defining a pattern. Patterns can be saved by using the Preset Manager, selecting the new patterns, and clicking Save Set.

KEY CONCEPT

edit>stroke   *stroke layer style*

strokes

p. 9

Add a stroke as a layer style or by using Edit>Stroke. Use a layer style to edit the stroke at any time, and the stroke automatically resizes as the layer resizes. Use Edit>Stroke to be able to apply filters to a stroke on a layer. Typically strokes should be set to Inside.

Adobe® Photoshop® TV

Get the latest insider Photoshop techniques, tips, and news from "The Photoshop Guys" themselves: Scott Kelby, Dave Cross, and Matt Kloskowski of the National Association of Photoshop Professionals (NAPP). If you're as passionate about Photoshop as we are, check it out every Monday in the iTunes Music Store or at **www.photoshoptv.com**.

The National Association of Photoshop Professionals (NAPP) is the world's most complete resource for Adobe® Photoshop® training, education, and news. As a NAPP member, you get a subscription to *Photoshop User* magazine, which has all of the top Photoshop gurus in the industry writing for it, including two columns by Dave Cross. You also get access to the members-only website (where Dave hosts weekly Quicktime-based tutorials), online Help Desk, great discounts, and so much more. NAPP also conducts live one-day Photoshop Training Seminars, and twice yearly hosts four days worth of classes at the Photoshop World Conference & Expo. Check it out at **www. photoshopuser.com**.

Books and Training DVDs

Check out **www.photoshopvideos.com** and **www.scottkelbybooks.com** for Dave's other titles, including *The Photoshop CS2 Help Desk Book*, *Illustrator CS2 Killer Tips*, and a host of invaluable training DVDs.

And More...

If that's not enough for you, Dave Cross also hosts a blog at **www.davecross.blogspot.com**.

blending options

p. 24

Found in the Layer Style dialog, you can get to it by choosing Blending Options from the Add a Layer Style pop-up menu or by double-clicking on the layer. In the Blend If section, use the This Layer slider to affect the visibility of the current layer, and use the Underlying Layer slider to make the bottom layer show through the current layer. Use the Option (PC: Alt) key to split the slider for a softer transition.

layer styles

p. 29

Layer styles add effects that are easy to edit and are completely scalable—and can be reused in other documents by saving as a Style. To copy a layer style from one layer to another, hold down the Option (PC: Alt) key and drag-and-drop the layer style icon. Use the Eye icons to the left of each layer style to hide or show the effects.

threshold

p. 32

The Threshold command converts a photo into a black-and-white pattern of pixels that can be used to define a brush or a pattern, or can be used as a border. Move the slider to determine the amount of black or white pixels you want. Threshold is available from the Image>Adjustments menu or as an adjustment layer.

Keyboard Shortcuts:

Layers

Press Command-J (PC: Control-J) to duplicate a layer.

Command-click (PC: Control-click) on the Create a New Layer icon to add a new layer below the current layer.

Press Shift-+ to scroll down through layer blend modes.

Layer Masks

Shift-click on the mask icon to show or hide the mask.

Option-click (PC: Alt-click) to view the layer mask.

Option-click (PC: Alt-click) on the Add Layer Mask icon to add the mask in black.

Press Command-I (PC: Control-I) to Invert the mask.

Painting/Color

Press] to increase brush size.

Press [to decrease brush size.

Press D for default colors (black Foreground, white Background).

Press X to swap Foreground and Background.

Press Option-Delete (PC: Alt-Backspace) to fill with the Foreground color.

Press Command-Delete (PC: Control-Backspace) to fill with the Background color.

Selections

Press-and-hold the Shift key to add to a selection.

Press-and-hold the Option (PC: Alt) key to remove from a selection.

Command-click (PC: Control-click) on the layer thumbnail to load a selection of the layer contents.

KEY CONCEPT

free transform

p. 10

Press Command-T (PC: Control-T) or use Edit>Free Transform to get the transformation handles. Click-and-drag on the handles, or use the settings in the Options Bar to resize numerically. Shift: keeps the transformation proportional; Option (PC: Alt): transforms from the center outwards; Command (PC: Control): transforms the one handle you click on; Command-Shift (PC: Control-Shift): skews; Command-Option-Shift (PC: Control-Alt-Shift): creates perspective; or move just outside the handles to get the Rotate cursor.

filters

p. 11

If nothing is selected, a filter will apply to the entire image or layer, so if you want to restrict the effects of a filter, make a selection first. If a filter has a Preview option, take advantage of it to compare "before" and "after." To reapply the last filter with the same settings, press Command-F (PC: Control-F). To open the dialog of the last filter you used so you can change the settings, press Command-Option-F (PC: Control-Alt-F).

blend modes

p. 13

Blend modes change the way the color used by a tool or layer interacts with the colors of the layer(s) below (a blend mode menu also appears in many layer styles). To scroll through the blend modes, press Shift-+. If you have a painting tool selected, you'll change the blend mode of that tool; if you have the Move tool selected, you'll scroll through the blend mode for the current active layer. (To scroll "backwards" through the blend modes, press Shift--.)

illustrator to photoshop

p. 19

Copy from Illustrator and Paste in Photoshop and choose from the options: Smart Object (creates a live, editable link to the Illustrator artwork); Pixels (creates a rasterized version of the vector artwork); Path (creates a work path in the Photoshop document); Shape Layer (creates a Shape layer that preserves the vector shape that can be edited).

adjustment layers

p. 22

Apply adjustments as an editable layer, giving you the ability to return to the original adjustment dialog to make further changes, hide it, delete it completely, change its opacity or blend mode, or include more than one of the same type of adjustment. Adjustment layers automatically include a layer mask.